BIG BETS GONE BAD

Derivatives
and
Bankruptcy
in
Orange County

PHILIPPE JORION

with the assistance of Robert Roper

Academic Press
San Diego   New York   Boston   London
Sydney   Tokyo   Toronto

Academic Press, Inc.
A Division of Harcourt Brace & Company
525 B Street, Suite 1900, San Diego, California 92101-4495

United Kingdom Edition published by
Academic Press Limited
24-28 Oval Road, London NW1 7DX

Library of Congress Cataloging-in-Publication Data

Jorion, Philippe, date.
    Big bets gone bad : derivatives and bankruptcy in Orange County /
by Philippe Jorion, with the assistance of Robert Roper.
        p.   cm.
    Includes bibliographical references and index.
    ISBN 0-12-390360-2
    1. Investment of public funds--California--Orange County.
2. Derivative securities. 3. Depts, public--California--Orange
County. 4. Municipal bankruptcy--California--Orange County.
5. Citron, Robert L. I. Roper, Robert. II. Title.
HJ3835.C3J67   1995
336.794'96--dc20   95-35120
                                                    CIP

PRINTED IN THE UNITED STATES OF AMERICA
95   96   97   98   99   00   MM   9   8   7   6   5   4   3   2   1

To my wife Dominique.

Contents

Prologue
· · · · · · · · · · · ·

This book describes how the collapse of the Orange County Investment Pool led to $1.7 billion in losses. I decided to write this book because I have two perspectives on the matter. First, as a resident of the City of Irvine with children in the city's school system, I share the strong feelings that this financial crisis has generated among county residents (my share of this loss is $3,500). Second, as a finance professor at the University of California at Irvine, I teach a class on derivatives and have some expertise in investments. In December I spent hours on the telephone talking to reporters and became quickly familiar with the detailed circumstances of this affair. But it is my wife who gave me the idea to write this book. She asked a basic question that is still troubling many Orange County residents: she couldn't understand how anyone could lose so much money.

This municipal debacle has also revealed a glaring need for better understanding of financial markets. The purpose of this book, therefore, is to offer a story that is both entertaining and informative. The lessons of this story, another example of California's eccentricities, should be useful reading for anybody dealing, directly or indirectly, with financial markets. Although not involved with the participants of this story, I feel free to offer an objective, if opinionated, interpretation of what happened. Here it is . . .

Irvine, California
May 1995

1

Introduction

· · · · · · · · · · · · · · · ·

Thursday December 1, 1994
Caller: *Professor Jorion, this is the Washington Post. Have you heard that the Orange County Investment Pool has lost $1.5 billion?*
Jorion: *That's nothing to be alarmed about. A $1.5 million loss is minor compared to the size of the pool.*
Caller: *That's not $1.5 million, Professor. It's $1.5 billion . . .*

· ·

O range County, California's announcement of a loss of $1.5 billion in its municipal investment pool sent shock waves across the country. In short order, Robert L. Citron, the county treasurer and reputed financial wizard, meekly agreed to resign, and the county declared itself bankrupt. It was the largest municipal failure in the history of the United States.

How big is $1.5 billion? (The loss amount was soon revised upward to $1.7 billion.) This is a sum greater than the annual Gross Domestic Product (GDP) of many small nations—Mozambique's GDP, for instance, is only around $1 billion. Or, to think about it another way, if the Orange County Supervisors were to put aside a dollar a second around the clock, they could wipe out their debt in a mere 54 years.

Or from another perspective, if 1.7 billion dollar bills were laid end to end, they would encircle the earth more than six times, a distance of about 260,000 kilometers (160,000 miles). That $1.7 billion is also what 70,000 adult Americans earn in a given year—roughly equal to all the salaries of all the people employed in Sacramento.

Also, $1.7 billion is close to the total market value of a large corporation, for instance, Bethlehem Steel. It represents a loss of $700 for every man, woman, and child in Orange County or roughly $2500 for the average household. A $1.7 billion loss, if absorbed by the county alone, will reduce municipal revenues in years to come by an amount equal to the interest payments foregone. At current rates, this translates into an annual shortfall of $100 million, computed forever.

On the other hand, Orange County is also one of the nation's wealthiest counties. Total real estate value is estimated at $100–150 billion. Annual production of goods and services exceeds that of many countries. Table 1.1 shows that the Orange County "Gross Regional Product," $74 billion in 1993, is larger than the GDP of Portugal, Israel, or Singapore. Indeed, Orange County by itself is the 30th largest economic power in the world.

Furthermore, Orange County has a vibrant economy, one that should be strong enough to shake off the effects of the December loss. As of late 1994, the local unemployment rate was below 5%, significantly lower than the U.S. average. Sometimes called *Silicon Valley South*, Orange County has a strong entrepreneurial base and an international reputation

Table 1.1

Orange County's Economy

	GDP in 1993, $ billions
United States	$6378
Japan	$4216
Germany	$1713
France	$1253
California	$750
Mexico	$329
Belgium	$211
Orange County	$74
Portugal	$71
Israel	$66
Singapore	$56

for high-tech innovation. It enjoys a modern infrastructure, a good public school system, a low crime rate, and an attractive climate and geography. The county is also uniquely positioned to benefit from growing trade links with Mexico and the Pacific Basin.

Seen in the context of these advantages, a loss of $1.7 billion looks steep but survivable. Other municipalities, however, should they sustain comparable losses, may not fare so well. For this reason alone, it may be useful to take a closer look at the Orange County fiasco.

Speaking the Dreaded *D* Word: Derivatives as Tools of the Devil

One intriguing aspect of the bankruptcy is how it touches on so many topics of current concern. Chief among these may be that category of financial instruments known as *derivatives*. The word *derivative* appeared in *Wall Street Journal* headlines only 8 times in 1992; in 1993, it appeared 28 times; in 1994, 128 times. Derivatives are widely believed to be the "cause" of the Orange County bankruptcy, as well as of the more recent collapse of the venerable British investment bank of Barings PLC.

Wall Street wise man Felix Rohatyn, speaking of derivatives, has warned that "26 year-olds with computers are creating financial hydrogen bombs." Henry Gonzalez, former House Banking Committee chairman, has described derivatives as "a monstrous global electronic Ponzi scheme." And the CBS TV show *60 Minutes*, in a March 1995 broadcast, claimed that derivatives were "too complicated to explain, but too important to ignore."

The show *60 Minutes* also said that derivatives are "highly exotic, little understood, and virtually unregulated . . . [they] make up a $35 trillion worldwide market . . . some people believe they're so unpredictable they could bring down the world banking system."

To make sense of the Orange County bankruptcy, this book will need to take a close look at derivatives. We will also examine other aspects of the bond (or fixed-income) market; we will discuss Treasury, agency, and mortgage-backed securities, including structured notes. No background in finance is required of the reader. Students of finance, however, may find the Orange County experience illuminating, because it touches on so many features of the current financial environment.

This book will endeavor to answer such questions as these:

- How can a municipal investment pool, supposedly safe, lose billions of dollars? What strategies caused such a loss?

- Are the funds controlled by your local government secure? What questions should you ask of government agencies making investments on your behalf?
- Do you, as a private investor, have instruments in your portfolio that could lead to dramatic losses? Are there derivatives hidden in assets you already own?
- Are derivatives always mad, bad, and dangerous to know? Is regulation the answer? Prohibition? Something else?

In Chapter 2, we take a look at the Orange County bankruptcy as a historical event. Robert L. Citron, the Orange County treasurer–tax collector, is central to what happened; and we will discuss his personality and his position within the county power structure.

In Chapters 3 through 8, we take a look at the financial instruments behind the crisis: bonds, repurchase agreements, derivatives, and other such creatures. As these chapters are essential to understanding the $1.7 billion loss, these topics are made as intuitive as possible. Impatient readers could skip directly to Chapter 9 and perhaps return to these chapters later. Remember, however, that the bankruptcy occurred precisely because of the lack of understanding of these financial instruments. As a reference for the reader, a glossary of financial terms is provided at the end of the text.

In Chapter 9 (and other chapters following it), we return to the Orange County story. What was Robert Citron's investment strategy? How did it lead to bankruptcy, and what are the short- and long-term effects? What about the legal aspects of the bankruptcy; what role, for example, did Merrill Lynch, the investment house, play? Who bears responsibility, legally and otherwise, for what happened?

In Chapters 15–18, we draw some conclusions from the Orange County experience. We will ask: how is risk to be

assessed for municipal investors and is there a need for closer
regulation of certain markets and for better disclosure?

Our hope is that this book will prove useful to general
readers, students of finance, and participants in pension
funds and investment pools of all kinds. Nobody likes to lose
$1.7 billion—there should be no reason for it to happen
again, at least not in this way.

2

Robert Citron and His World

· ·

"This is a person who has gotten us millions of dollars. I don't know how in the hell he does it, but it makes us all look good."
ORANGE COUNTY SUPERVISOR THOMAS RILEY, APRIL 1994

· ·

I n June 1994, Robert Citron won election to a seventh term as Orange County treasurer–tax collector, with a majority over 60%. Citron, 69 years old at the time, had been for many years the only important elected Democrat in a famously Republican bastion. Orange County is the birthplace of Richard Nixon; in 1980 and 1984, the county gave Ronald Reagan his largest margins of victory nationwide.

Citron was a unique figure in local politics. For 24 years he ruled the county treasury, supervising tax collection and the investment of county funds. The Orange County Investment Pool (OCIP) amassed revenues from 187 public bodies, including cities and school districts, water authorities and sanitation districts, and pension funds. It was Citron's responsibility to invest these monies, amounting to $7.5 billion in

1994, subject to the requirements of state law and the oversight of a five-member Board of Supervisors.

Citron, who never earned a college degree—and who described himself, postbankruptcy, as "inexperienced" and "not as sophisticated as I thought I was"—racked up an astonishing early record as county treasurer. Under his stewardship, the OCIP earned an average return on investment of 9.4% per annum. Even during the recent recession, OCIP delivered yields of 8–9%, even though the California treasury averaged only 5–6%. This differential amounted to additional profits for the county of $500 million in the period 1991–93 alone.

Citron's success attracted national attention. In 1988, *City & State* magazine named him one of the five best financial officers in the country. In Orange County he could do no wrong: in a militantly tax-averse political environment, he produced enormous revenues "painlessly," thus allowing government to function and expand. In December 1993, the Board of Supervisors honored him for generating sufficient surplus revenues to bankroll a major new gang-suppression program. Ronald Rubino, former Orange County budget director, said that he would "like to clone [Citron] and use him to head some of our other departments."

In the course of his long run of financial success, Citron built an extraordinary personal fiefdom. The Supervisors mostly left him alone to do his "wizardry" (although in the wake of the bankruptcy, some have said they were not given adequate information about his activities). When criticized for his management of county investments, he responded heatedly and sometimes viciously. For example, Goldman, Sachs & Co., in October 1993, criticized some of his market maneuvers. Citron wrote back that Goldman officials "don't understand the type of investment strategies that we are using. . . . I would suggest that you not seek doing business" with Orange County. In 1992, when a local employee of the brokerage firm A. G. Edwards & Son, Mark Robles, dared question Citron's investment policies, Citron wrote directly to Ben Edwards, the company chairman, in tones of injured majesty claiming that "Many of [Robles's] statements are libelous to the Orange County treasurer."

Perhaps the most cogent, most thorough critique of Citron's investment strategy emerged during the 1994 election. John Moorlach, a certified public accountant and financial planner, made Citron's policies the central issue of his campaign; and his arguments—resoundingly rejected by the voters—make eery reading now. Moorlach said that "Mr. Citron believes he can accurately anticipate the market all the time, and also outperform everyone. That's impossible." Moorlach also characterized the OC portfolio as "a major bull-market bet in the middle of a bear market." Just before the election itself, early in June, Moorlach claimed that Citron's strategies had caused the portfolio to decline in value by an astonishing $1.2 billion. "The incumbent has structured the portfolio . . . on the premise that interest rates would continue to decline," a fundamental—and disastrous—mistake.

Citron, unopposed in six previous elections, treated Moorlach's attacks as mere partisan propaganda. He seemed offended that anyone would dare question his investment program, which had proven so successful. Furthermore, Citron and his allies repeatedly attacked Moorlach for being "like a guy who runs into a theater and yells 'Fire!'" His criticisms were undermining the county's standing on Wall Street, they maintained, which would make it harder to borrow money in the future (e.g., through bond issues). "It's like somebody passing on false information about a financial institution," Citron said, "causing a run on the bank."

In the end, Citron won the election. But Moorlach lived to see his uncanny predictions come true, each and every one. Or were his predictions really so "uncanny"? Was the

Orange County bankruptcy a fiasco that any objective observer, given a basic familiarity with financial affairs, might have foretold? And if it was predictable, then why did this disastrous bankruptcy have to happen?

. . . .

"There's nothing worse than a gambler who goes to Vegas and wins the first time."
                     CHRISS STREET, ORANGE COUNTY REPUBLICAN ACTIVIST

. . . .

The son of a medical doctor, Robert Citron, a third-generation Californian, grew up in Burbank and in the outlying town of Hemet, where his family moved to escape the smog. Robert's father, Jesse, treated the alcoholic comedian W. C. Fields and is reputed to have weaned him off scotch. When Dr. Citron billed Fields, however, after a long course of treatment, the entertainer sued him; Fields eventually lost in court, and he would later claim that Dr. Citron was the only man ever to best him at anything.

Robert, who had been asthmatic as a child, hoped to become a physician like his father. After two years of pre-med at USC, however, he switched to business, then left school several semesters short of a degree. (In the 1950s he studied government finance at Loyola, again without taking a degree.) As an officer of the privately held Century Finance Corporation, Citron made consumer loans but eventually presided over the liquidation of the company. In 1960 he joined the staff of the Orange County tax collector. Here he rose to the position of supervisor. In 1971, upon the retirement of the sitting tax collector, Citron ran for office and won.

In the early 1970s, Orange County was less Republican, less economically dynamic than it would soon become. The

GOP old guard, closely identified with commerce and agriculture, was being challenged by a nascent Democratic machine and by high-powered real estate and manufacturing interests. Citron emerged as a political figure at a time when professional managers were taking over in the public sector, led by a City Hall clique controlled by Louis Cella, head of a medical clinic in Santa Ana. (Dr. Cella and many of his associates went to jail later in the 1970s.) Though never implicated in Cella's criminal activities, Citron was closely associated with Cella and learned a personal style of politics and favor-trading that would mark his behavior for the rest of his public career.

Registered Democrats briefly outnumbered registered Republicans in Orange County, but by the end of the 1970s, the county had emerged as the conservative stronghold it remains today. Citron would thereafter be increasingly isolated as a partisan politician. However, he secured his position as Treasurer—indeed, made himself almost invulnerable to challenge—by performing well in office and fighting back all attempts to oversee his operations. At least three times during his tenure, independent agencies recommended greater outside scrutiny of his investment practices. Citron undermined these efforts by arguing that a financial officer needed wide latitude to maximize market opportunities, and his remarkable success seemed to justify this philosophy.

Citron also began a campaign to relax the laws that govern municipal investors. Throughout the late 1970s–early 1980s, he lobbied hard for changes in state regulations; and eventually the California legislature liberalized the statutes that pertain to county treasuries. Thereafter, officials like Citron could invest in more exotic instruments—for example, in "reverse repurchase" agreements (a type of financial product explained in a later chapter).

Having increased his scope as an investor—"I'm the one that wrote the legislation to make these types of investment possible," he liked to brag—Citron became more powerful and more essential to the economic functioning of the county. To understand his increasing importance and independence, we need to look briefly at economic conditions in California at the time of Citron's rise.

Jarvis–Gann and the Tax Revolt

Beginning with the Oil Crisis of 1973, then throughout the remainder of the decade, inflation combined with a shift in property tax burdens to make conditions ever worse for individual homeowners. In California, state and local taxes were unusually high by U.S. standards, and demographic changes were producing an electorate with less commitment to issues such as public education and more concern for the erosion of fixed incomes.

Howard Jarvis, a retired businessman and conservative reformer, had spent over 10 years leading unsuccessful anti-tax crusades. In 1978, though, the Jarvis–Gann Initiative, which he coauthored, led to the passage of Proposition 13, which drastically changed property tax collection in California. The tax rate was set at no more than 1% of assessed value, and properties not sold since 1976 were assessed at their fair market value for that year. Other provisions of Proposition 13 required that new taxes or increases be approved by a two-thirds vote of the state legislature (or for local taxes, by a two-thirds popular majority).

Thus, at a time of rapid population growth and concomitant increases in the demand on public services, California counties found their access to revenues severely restricted. Howard Jarvis and his supporters had always been opposed to government services: Jarvis, in his years of antitax campaigning, had attacked Social Security, Medicare, and public financing for parks, schools, libraries, and garbage collection. Now a conservative opposition to government programs hitched its star to the widespread resentment of property taxes, with the result that local governments, especially in high-growth areas like Orange County, were caught in an ever-worsening fiscal squeeze.

Against this background Robert Citron, who could "magically" secure the revenues for an expanding government, first came into prominence. Personally conservative, conscientious to a fault, and penurious—he was famous for divvying up lunch tabs on his wristwatch calculator—Citron was uncommonly adventurous when it came to investing public funds. Although only sketchily educated in finance, he "learned on the job" (as he later claimed) and showed an unusual appreciation of the opportunities presented by the 1980s–1990s bond market. No one has ever accused Citron of personal dishonesty or of trying to enrich himself. Married to the same woman for 39 years, he lived in a modest house in Santa Ana and subsisted quite happily, toward the end of his career, on a yearly salary of $100,339. He claimed never to have owned a single share of stock; and he neither drank, smoked, nor gambled. A notoriously hard worker, Citron could rarely be persuaded to take a vacation: "He can barely stand the weekend at home," his wife once told a reporter. "He can't wait to get back [to the office]."

Citron's eccentricities, regarded with affection by most of his peers, were recognizably Southern Californian. In his early years he liked to dress in white belts, plaid slacks, and oddly colored sports coats; as he grew older he preferred ordinary business clothes, but he accented his wardrobe with ostentatious displays of Amerindian turquoise jewelry. His car horn played the fight song of the University of Southern California, and his bathroom was painted the USC colors, cardinal and gold. His desk at the county treasurer's office, boldly adorned with a bronzed lump of horse manure (courtesy of "Traveler," the USC mascot), was clearly a locus of municipal power: other county workers found him prickly, secretive, controlling, decisive, and arrogant. "He's one of our better administrators and I respect him," said Shirley Grindle, a county activist, "but I think he's gotten a little cocky from all those years in office." Many commented on his defensiveness: when criticized, Citron's tendency was to launch fierce counterattacks or to bluster.

How much Citron knew about municipal investing, and how much he only thought he knew, is very much in question. His annual reports to the Board of Supervisors were rambling and incoherent. (That he reported on a yearly basis is in itself amazing. Assets under management increased eightfold at OCIP in the period 1988–94, to a whopping $7.4 billion. Managers of much smaller funds frequently report to overseers on a quarterly or even a monthly basis.) Puzzled by Citron's verbal presentations, the Board of Supervisors asked for written reports, but these were equally incomprehensible. For example, in the report of September 26, 1994, Citron wrote, "We do not have the large inflationary wage increases, runaway building, both in homes, commercial, and those tall glass office buildings. . . . Few, if any, tall office buildings are being built." After the bankruptcy, other county officers recalled that Citron's explanations were self-serving; one remembered that he was "basically blowing [his] own horn" in the reports he submitted.

When asked, late in 1993, why he believed interest rates would remain low, Citron replied: "I am one of the largest investors in America. I know these things." It appears that Citron took his cue on interest rates from figures such as Charles Clough, Jr., the chief investment strategist at Merrill Lynch, who has an excellent reputation on the street. Clough predicted (incorrectly) that rates would stay low throughout the decade; and when the Fed began instituting rate hikes in February 1994, Clough seriously underestimated the levels they would rise to. Citron also took market advice from brokers, such as Merrill's Michael Stamenson, who were interested mainly in selling more investments to OCIP. As with all brokers, Stamenson's performance as prognosticator cum salesman reflects the conflict of interest inherent in his function. In any event, Citron appears to have violated some basic tenets of common sense, and his image as a "knowledgeable insider" appears largely fanciful.

For all his arrogance, Citron was painfully uncomfortable with strangers. By all reports he preferred the company of loyal friends, such as the old cronies he lunched with every day at the Santa Ana Elks' Club. In the early 1990s, his investment success became even more important to Orange County: property values had begun to fall, thus further reducing tax revenues, which led of necessity to greater reliance on the earnings of the OCIP. Between fiscal 1992 and 1993, the share of income from interest-bearing investments rose from 3% to 35% of the budget, while the property tax percentage fell from 60% to 25%. Although enjoying phenomenal success, Citron must have felt great pressure both personally and professionally: the fate of the county seemed to rest ever more in his hands alone.

The Impact of the Moorlach Campaign

Isolated from outside criticism and psychologically defended against competing points of view, Citron pursued his investment strategy throughout 1993 and into 1994. When John Moorlach, the Costa Mesa accountant, decided to challenge him in the June election, Citron was sincerely surprised. By all accounts, he took the challenge as a personal affront, almost as an attack on his honor. After all, he had been the best performing municipal investor in California for over 20 years—Orange County's acknowledged savior.

Moorlach, a newspaper columnist and host of *The Costa Mesa Conservative Report*, a cable TV show, proved a determined and informed opponent. Interest rates began to rise in February, and Moorlach publicly noted the risk to the OCIP, which was highly leveraged and invested in rate-sensitive structured securities. (Citron's investment strategy will be discussed in detail in following chapters.) A Moorlach supporter, Chriss Street, contacted the *Wall Street Journal*, *Forbes* magazine, and Standard & Poor's Ratings Group in New York, to draw attention to the OCIP's interest rate exposure. As a result, articles began to appear that questioned Citron's management plan. *The Wall Street Journal* likened his strategy to the practices that led to the savings and loan scandal. A financial trade publication, *Bond Buyer*, declared that OCIP was "heading to a nasty business"; and another journal, *Derivatives Week*, called the Orange County situation "a scandal waiting to happen."

It is not clear how going to Wall Street would have attracted additional votes, but there was an immediate backlash in the county. Political forces, Republican as well as Democrat, lined up solidly behind Citron, and he was never in serious danger of losing to Moorlach. All five county supervisors endorsed him, as did the *Los Angeles Times* and the *Orange County Register*. Still, Citron feared the effects of so much outside scrutiny; he accused Moorlach of making "dangerous" statements that could damage the county's credit rating, which in turn would force participants in OCIP—all those school districts, cities, and other public agencies that contributed their revenues—to pay millions more to borrow in the future. He declared publicly that this would be his last election and that, if he won, it would be his last term in office. "My wife and I have a very loving relationship," he explained, "and I'm not going to put her through this again. [It] tears her up."

A year later, Citron's assistant treasurer, Matthew Raabe, recalled that "the election . . . turned [Citron] into a very fragile man. He was an imposing and dominating figure all throughout the county for many, many, many years and by November he was this frail old man." Others claimed that Citron was so upset by Moorlach's challenge that he could hardly talk about it; he began coming to work later in the morning and leaving earlier in the afternoon, and a long-time habit of whistling quietly to himself through his teeth became exaggerated.

The county clerk, Gary Granville, an old friend of Citron, recalls that he became badly stooped over, "as if he were physically withdrawing and making himself smaller." Clearly, Moorlach's criticisms were hitting home: though they failed to carry the election for Moorlach, they precipitated a crisis in Citron's personality. Ideas that he overtly denied—but whose validity he perhaps unconsciously recognized—were beginning to trouble him, and in the end the pressure undermined his health and confidence. In his annual report to the county supervisors, delivered September 26, he defended his philosophy and career in his usual rambling way, but also admitting that he had failed to anticipate recent sharp interest rate increases. Quoting George Bernard Shaw and Harry Truman, he assured the supervisors that the county had suffered only "paper" losses, however, and that fiscal 1994 would prove profitable in the end.

By late October, when Assistant Treasurer Raabe was discussing OCIP's problems with county administrators, Citron was increasingly out of touch. He was in "a state of denial over this," Raabe has said. "It didn't seem like he was facing reality." Raabe has also claimed that Citron began consulting a psychic and a mail-order astrologer at work. But the problem was not in the stars, but rather in the brokerage houses and investment banks on Wall Street. They, too, were now aware of the untenability of OCIP's investment position, and several refused to roll over their loans to the county. On December 1, 1994, the Board of Supervisors officially announced a $1.5 billion loss in the fund. Less than a week later, after frantic attempts to sell the damaged portfolio came to nothing, Orange County declared itself bankrupt.

On December 4, a Sunday, Raabe and several other county officials visited Citron at home. "He just looked extremely sad, befuddled," Raabe has said. "You can imagine a man who has run a portfolio for 20 something years, having people come in and say the loss has turned into a real loss and this is going to be the end of your career." After a few minutes, Citron agreed to sign a letter of resignation. Two women officials, Eileen Walsh and Lynne Fishel, stayed behind with Citron, awaiting the arrival of a psychiatric social worker, while the rest of the delegation returned glumly to City Hall.

3

Bond Basics

. . . .

The Orange County Investment Pool handled funds on behalf of almost 200 different public bodies. It accepted cash surpluses and tax revenues from these organizations, and it provided payouts as required to meet their operational needs.

Are local government investment pools a good idea? Generally speaking, yes. Just as small investors enjoy benefits from mutual funds, which pool the contributions of thousands of other such investors, municipalities benefit from economies of scale when they join their revenues in a single fund. Presumably, they also enjoy the benefits of expert fund management.

A large investment pool can use its clout to get better deals. It negotiates better prices from the brokers who handle its transactions, and it may also have access to a wider choice of investments. The management fee charged OCIP was 7 basis points (0.07%), which amounted to about $5 million in 1993. A smaller fund would have paid a rate of about 30 basis points.

Because such pools serve the operational needs of government agencies, they need to be managed conservatively. If the investment horizon is short, the funds should be invested to pose no risk at all to principal. If the funds can be left in place for a longer time period, the fund can be managed like a short-term bond fund—again, with little risk to principal.

Some pools, however—and not only Orange County's—have been following more aggressive investment strategies. They take large interest rate bets, or they invest in derivatives and mortgages, perhaps without a full understanding of the risks involved. A recent survey by the Government Finance Officers Association revealed that only 4% of its members said they were knowledgeable about derivatives; 76% said they had only some or no knowledge. Without a proper understanding, as we will soon see, dealing in derivatives is an invitation to disaster.

One factor that disposed some pools to become more aggressive was the historically low level of interest rates in 1993 (around 3%). Municipalities, used to 5–7% annual returns, tried various means to pump up their yield. As we shall see, an addiction to high yields became more and more dangerous when it involved additional exposure to market risk.

In February 1994, the Fed instituted the first of six interest rate increases for the year. These hikes led to huge losses in the bond market: in 1994, more wealth was wiped off balance sheets than in any other market debacle since the Crash of 1929. Some supposedly safe municipal investment pools also suffered. Although Orange County is in a league of its own, Table 3.1 shows that many municipalities across the country took big losses.

These serious losses have prompted calls for stricter oversight of investment pools, along with bans on the use of derivatives and leverage. To understand the Orange County failure, we need, first, to analyze the mechanics of the bond market.

Table 3.1

Recent Losses in Public Funds

	Assets ($ million)	Loss ($ million)	Loss (%)
Orange County, CA	7,400	1,690	22%
San Diego, CA	3,300	357	11%
West Virginia State	1,200	279	23%
Florida State Treasury	8,000	200	3%
Cuyahoga County, OH	1,800	137	8%
Texas State	3,700	55	1%
City Colleges of Chicago	96	48	50%
Placer County, CA	378	26	7%
Escambia County, FL	101	25	25%
Charles County, MD	30	24	20%
San Bernardino County, CA	338	16	5%
City of Auburn, MN	17	7	40%

And we need to familiarize ourselves with the financial instruments that Robert Citron used in his investment program.

. . . .

Congratulations, you just won a $100 savings bond!
Thanks. How much is that worth if I sell it now?
Well—about $50.

. . . .

This example illustrates a mysterious aspect of fixed-income investments such as bonds: because the principal, or face, value ($100) is to be paid in the future, the current, or market, value is quite different ($50). The market value is the price at which buyers and sellers would willingly trade the bond, and it reflects current conditions in the market.

The difference between the face and market values reflects the *time value* of money. Because inflation erodes the value of a dollar, receiving $100 now is preferable to receiving $100 in the future (18 years off in the case of a typical savings bond). And money now can be put to work.

This difference leads to much confusion, which is often exploited for sales purposes. For instance, consider junk mail invitations to enter a typical sweepstakes lottery, with a prize of $10 million. This prize, should you be lucky enough to win it, would be paid out over 30 years in annual installments of $333,333. By judiciously spreading out the payments, the *market* value of the prize, discounted at 8%, is really $4,909,074. Not bad—but different!

Although face value is easy to assess, market value is a more complicated matter. Sometimes the difference is not appreciated. For example, Robert Citron maintained, right up until December 6 (when Orange County declared itself bankrupt), that OCIP had incurred only "paper" losses; that is, losses that would go on the books only if the county's creditors sold the securities they had taken as collateral. The logic behind this argument is that, if held to maturity, securities bring their full face value in the market. The problem is that, as in our savings bond example, $100 in 18 years may be worth only $50 now. And Orange County's creditors were decidedly *not* willing to wait to sell.

Valuing Bonds

The OCIP was invested in fixed-income securities. A fixed-income security is a government, corporate, or municipal bond that pays a fixed rate of interest until the bond matures, at which time the issuer pays the full face value. When the bonds are short-term, with maturity less than 10 years, they can be called *notes*.

The essential feature of a fixed-income security is that the coupon payments and face value are fixed for the life of

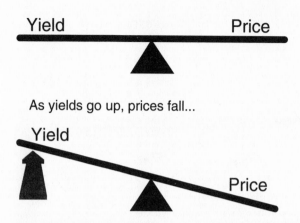

Figure 3.1. Bond Price and Yield

the bond. But even with a fixed face value, the *market* value of a bond can change through time. As market yields (interest rates) change, the sale price of a bond fluctuates, creating a potential for losses as well as profit opportunities for smart portfolio managers. (Remember, bonds can be sold to other investors before they mature.)

To understand why prices change, consider a 2-year, 4% note (4% paid annually) initially purchased at a price of $100 when interest rates were at 4%. Assume next that the Federal Reserve decides to increase rates to 5%. The unfortunate investor is now stuck with a note that pays a paltry 4%, when he or she could buy a new note paying 5%.

At the higher rate, the original note falls in market value; this fall represents the foregone opportunity of investing at the higher rate (5%). From the point of view of an economist, this loss is a true loss whether realized (cashed out) or not.

This type of loss, due to an increase in yields, is what led to the debacle at OCIP. Orange County was massively invested in fixed-income notes.

Thus, *increasing yields decrease the market value of a bond.* Figure 3.1 displays the inverse relationship between bond

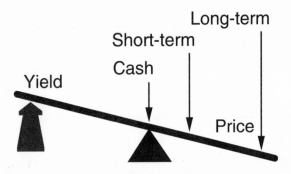

Figure 3.2. Bond Price and Maturity

price and yields, using the example of a seesaw that swings around a fulcrum.

The seesaw analogy also helps explain an essential aspect of the risk of fixed-income securities. *All else being equal, the price drop increases the longer the maturity of the original bond* (see Figure 3.2). This is because more cash flows (annual payments) are stuck at the paltry 4% coupon.

Figure 3.3 summarizes the effect of changes in interest rates in a hypothetical example with a starting rate of 5%. Note

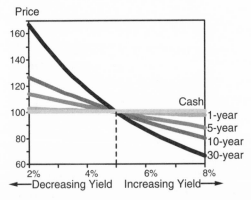

Figure 3.3. The Relationship between Prices and Yields

Percent Price Change

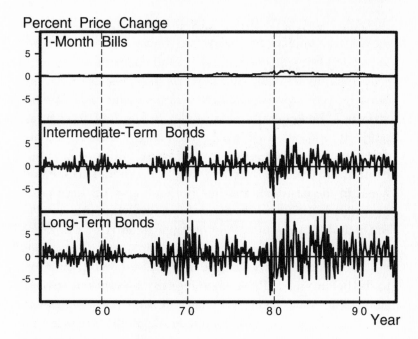

Figure 3.4. Risk in the Bond Market

the inverse relationship between bond price (market value) and yield. The longer the maturity of a bond, the greater is its susceptibility to changes in either direction in interest rates.

Risk

Longer maturities increase the risk of fixed-income instruments. Figure 3.4 displays the range of variation of monthly returns for different sectors of the fixed-income market, from 1953 to 1994. The cash sector is represented by a 1-month Treasury bill, the intermediate bond sector by a 5-year note, the long-term sector by a 20-year bond.

The figure shows dramatically how the variability of returns increases with maturity. The safest sector, Treasury bills, has low and stable returns. The intermediate sector has more variability, with an average movement of about 1–2% per month. The long-term sector has highly volatile returns, commonly reaching plus or minus 5% in one month.

Volatility tends to cluster across time. For example, the bond market experienced wild swings starting in 1979. This was when the Federal Reserve Bank, led by Paul Volcker, attempted to squash the high inflation plaguing the U.S. economy. The Fed jacked up short-term interest rates, which went from 9% in 1979 to over 16% two years later. This created havoc in the bond market, notably leading to the debt crisis of the early 1980s, when many developing nations, such as Brazil and Mexico, defaulted on their debt, largely because they could not meet higher interest payments.

The figure shows that the 1990s have been quieter, up to the beginning of 1994, when interest rates started upward again. The sharp increase in rates in the United States was also a factor leading to the recent devaluation of the Mexican peso, which nearly caused a financial collapse in that country.

The relative quiet of the early 1990s may have lulled some market participants into a false sense of security. Traders with long memories will recall that, in the 1960s, the worst quarterly loss on long-term bonds was −5.3%; in the 1970s, −8.4%; in the 1980s, −7.4%. The worst quarterly loss since 1990 occurred at the beginning of 1994, when returns reached −4.5%. This appears to be large by the standards of the 1990s, but is clearly within the norm of the past several decades.

Duration

We have seen that bonds with longer maturities display greater price movements. But maturity is an imperfect measure of risk: it only accounts for the repayment of principal. In fact, there will be many intervening coupon payments for a bondholder. *Duration* provides a better measure of price risk because it accounts for all payments, not just the principal.

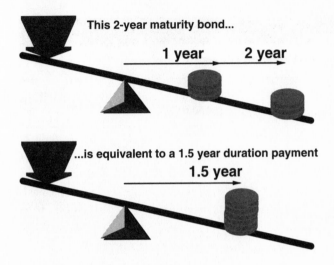

This 2-year maturity bond...

1 year   2 year

...is equivalent to a 1.5 year duration payment

1.5 year

Figure 3.5. Bond Price and Duration

Like maturity, duration is measured in number of years. Duration is generally less than maturity, except for bonds that pay no coupons (zero-coupon bonds), for which maturity equals duration. (Zero-coupon bonds arise when an investment bank buys regular bonds, then creates two synthetic securities, one receiving the interest payments, the other consisting of the principal. Such securities are called *separate trading of registered interest and principal of securities*, or STRIPs.) For some securities or with leverage, however, duration can be greater than the average portfolio maturity, as will be explained in the next chapter.

Duration can be intuitively defined as the average maturity of all payments, with each payment weighted by its value. Consider a bond that makes two payments, $50 in one year and another $50 at the end of two years. (This is just for the sake of argument: most bond coupon payments are much smaller than the principal.) The maturity of our bond is two years. But clearly, value will have been received before the end of the two years. Figure 3.5 extends the lever analogy to

Table 3.2

Maturity and Duration (years)

Maturity	Duration (6% coupon)	Duration (8% coupon)
1	0.99	0.98
2	1.91	1.89
3	2.79	2.73
5	4.39	4.22
7	5.82	5.49
10	7.66	7.07
30	14.25	11.76

this bond. Duration is measured by the average distance from the fulcrum, which is about one-and-a-half years.

To look at duration another way, a 30-year mortgage may have a *duration* of only 12 or 13 years. This means that the amount loaned may actually be paid back in less than half the time stipulated. Duration is a measure that seeks to answer the question, how long will it take to recover the market price, in present value terms, considering the average time required to collect all payments of principal and interest?

Table 3.2 shows the duration of a number of notes and bonds. Its calculation depends on the coupon payment and the prevailing interest rate. As the table shows, for a 6% coupon, the duration of a 10-year note is 7.66 years. With an 8% coupon, more is paid earlier, and the duration falls to 7.07 years.

Practitioners in the bond market use duration to measure the price risk of any fixed-income instrument. Duration measures the linear exposure of a bond to movements in yields. As such, it is a good measure of market risk. Gains and losses can be computed as follows.

Dollar Loss = Duration × Dollar Value × Increase in Yield

To see how effective duration can be to explain returns, consider the case of the OCIP. In October 1992, Merrill sent a letter to Citron, warning that, although the portfolio had an average maturity of only 1.4 years, its effective duration was *seven* years. The state auditor confirmed that OCIP's duration was 7.4 years when it went bankrupt. In 1994, short-term interest rates went up by about 3%. With a $7.5 billion portfolio, this implies a loss of 7 years times $7.5 billion times 0.03, which is $1.6 billion! This is what Moorlach was desperately trying to explain during his campaign.

But why was the duration so much higher than the average maturity? Essentially, because of repos.

4

Repos
· · · · · · · ·

"When you win, you win big.
When you lose, you also can lose big."

JOHN MOORLACH, APRIL 1994
· ·

A repurchase agreement—also known as a *repo*, or RP—is a financial instrument that played a major role in the Orange County portfolio. As we will see, repos created *leverage* and led to about $1 billion in losses for OCIP.

A repo is a contract between a seller and a buyer that stipulates the sale, and later repurchase, of securities at a particular date and price. A repo is essentially a short-term loan to the seller, with the securities used as collateral.

Imagine you need cash for one year. You sell title to your house to a bank in exchange for a loan, at the same time agreeing to repurchase the house in a year at a fixed price. This price includes the loan amount plus accrued interest. If you default on your loan, the bank takes possession of your house. This type of arrangement describes the essence of a repo.

The seller in a repurchase transaction is typically a securities dealer. A *reverse repo* is the same operation but seen from the other point of view, the buyer's. In a reverse repurchase transaction, the dealer (buyer) trades money for securities, agreeing to resell them later. Securities dealers, who hold large inventories of bonds, often use repos to amass additional funds. Although dealers customarily have large amounts of capital on hand, they may take positions many times in excess of their capital. Using their securities as collateral, they borrow using repos.

From the viewpoint of investors (buyers), repos are a way to "park" funds on a temporary basis. Repos offer an alternative to investing in short-term Treasury bills (issued by the government) or bank deposits (guaranteed by the issuing bank). Repos are actually safer than other short-term deposits. Uninsured bank deposits are always subject to the risk of default by the issuing bank. With a repo, an investor holds a security against such a default. This is why money market mutual funds, for instance, invest in repos.

The U.S. repo market is a creature of Federal Reserve Regulation Q, which went into effect March 31, 1986. Q prohibited banks from paying interest on deposits with a maturity of less than 30 days. "There's nothing like regulation to spur innovation," as the saying goes, and investors switched from bank deposits to making short-term loans against securities, thus gaining interest on idle cash balances. More than $500 billion worth of business is transacted in the U.S. repo market daily, which makes it an important source of liquidity for the bond market.

Types of Repos

The largest part of the market is the *overnight* repo market, where the duration of loans is one day. The *repo rate* is a key interest rate for short-term capital costs, determined by supply and demand for capital.

In the *open* repo market, investors lend to sellers for indeterminate periods according to loose, continuing contracts. The rate on open repos varies daily and is approximately the same as the overnight repo rate.

Term repos are transactions for specific periods of time at fixed rates that may differ from the overnight repo rate. Most of the OCIP repos were open or term repos, with average maturity from three to six months. The rate of interest on a term repo often depends on the security being loaned. If a particular bond is in great demand, a dealer may charge a lower rate of interest in exchange for acquiring this bond.

Leverage

Reverse repos played a major role in the downfall of the OCIP. To illustrate, let us consider a security that was actually held by the pool. On December 31, 1993, OCIP owned $100 million in face value of the June 1998 FNMA issue, with a coupon of 5.38%. The bond was being quoted (valued) at 100 plus 14/32, or 100.4375; that is, $100.4375 for every $100 in face value.

OCIP's strategy was to sell the bond to a dealer, such as Crédit Suisse First Boston (CSFB), agreeing to repurchase in 30 days at a fixed price. In the meantime, CSFB would sell the bond to another client. OCIP would receive cash in an amount slightly less than $100 million. (The amount by which collateral exceeds the loan value is called the *margin* or *haircut*. The margin, which is not a cost, but a cushion to protect the lender should the borrower default, is generally between 1% and 3% of the value of a loan for credit-worthy borrowers.) To simplify, let us assume that OCIP received $100 million in exchange for the bond.

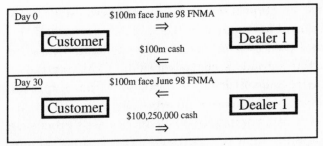

Figure 4.1. Example of a Reverse Repo

The dealer, of course, would require interest on the loan. This would be factored into the repurchase price. If the repo rate was 3%, the lender would require after 30 days

$$\$100 \text{ million} \times 3\% \times 30/360 = \$250,000$$

in interest. Payment at expiration would then be $100,250,000. Figure 4.1 summarizes the cash flows involved in the operation.

Why would anybody enter into this transaction? *Because it is profitable if interest rates go down or stay constant.* The bond pays a coupon that is higher than the repo rate. Assume the cash is reinvested in the same note. OCIP now holds $200 million of the FNMA note. If interest rates stay put, the investor receives the interest on the note, 5.38%, and pays 3% in interest, which is a net profit of about

$$\$100 \text{ million} \times (5.38\% - 3.00\%) \times 30/360 = \$198,333.$$

Not bad for a simple transaction. Perhaps this is why Raabe called repos "a slam dunk."

But why not repeat the process? Take the latest $100 million, enter another reverse repo with another dealer (call this one Dealer 2), and purchase another $100 million of the same issue. OCIP now holds $300 million of the FNMA note. The gain now goes to 2 x $198,333 = $396,667! In his August 28, 1991, annual report to the Board of Supervisors, Citron bragged that "We have perfected the reverse repo procedure to a new level."

Total Exposure ($300M) Leverage:	=	Initial Note ($100m) 3 to 1	+	First Reverse RP ($100m)	+	Second Reverse RP ($100m)

But wait. There has to be a catch! We have assumed that interest rates would not move. When entering a repo, the investor is still exposed to interest rate risk, even though one is lending out one's securities. This is because one reclaims title in a month. If yields go up, the value of the securities goes down.

And now—it gets even worse. By piling three purchases one on top of the other, the investor increases the exposure to three times the original amount. The initial $100 million has been leveraged into a total position of $300 million, for a *leverage ratio* of 3 to 1. If yields increase, such a strategy may lead to disaster. From December 1993 to November 1994, the yield on the issue in our example went from 5.24% to 7.88%, with a corresponding price drop of $100.44 to $92.34. Robert Citron had leveraged OCIP by a factor of three: enormous for a supposedly safe investment pool.

Figure 4.2 shows how the value of the investment varies with leverage. Investing in a 5-year note and adding two repos leads to a 3-to-1 leverage ratio. If yields increase by 1%, the

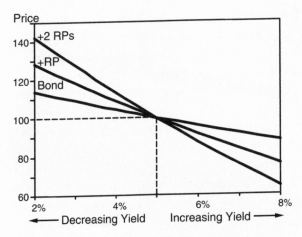

Figure 4.2. Reverse Repos: Value and Yield

note falls from $100.0 to $95.8; on the other hand, adding two repos leads to a drop in value to $87.4.

Now consider Figure 4.3, which describes repos and market exposure. This looks suspiciously like Figure 3.2,

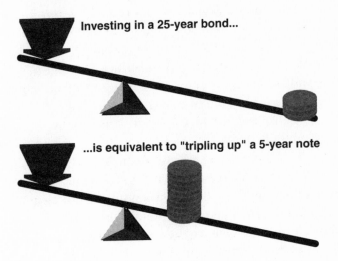

Figure 4.3. Reverse Repos and Market Risk

which showed that investing in longer term bonds increases the potential for gains and losses. As Figure 4.3 shows, investing in 5-year notes with a 3-to-1 leverage ratio is approximately equivalent to a straight investment in one 25-year bond. The duration of a 5-year note is 4.4 years, which translates into $3 \times 4.4 = 13.2$ years. This is roughly the duration of a bond with 25 years to maturity. *Repos multiply the effective portfolio duration by the leverage ratio.*

This helps explain the magnitude of the OCIP losses. A 20% loss seems extraordinary, but it is not—not for holders of long-term bonds. A 30-year bond loses about 15% of its value for every 1% increase in yield. Given that yields on long-term bonds went up from 6% to 8% in 1994, a loss of 20% of principal seems more than possible.

Margin Calls

A repo can be rolled over (i.e., extended or renewed) as long as both parties agree to do so. But if the value of the collateral falls, the lender will want some further guarantee and can (will) request that an additional amount of cash be put up. In our example, because the dealer has lent $100 million, and the value of the bond fell by more than $8 million, Dealer 1 will request that the investor produce $8 million in cash. But so will Dealer 2. Therefore, the investor will have to supply an additional $16 million to roll over the RPs.

Between February and May 1994, this is exactly what happened to the OCIP. To cover its loans, the fund had to put up some $515 million in cash. Between August and November of that year, OCIP's cash reserves shrank from $1.4 billion to about $350 million (the exact amount is not clear). Soon there was little left to meet collateral calls.

When investors fail to make the required additional payment, dealers have a right to liquidate the securities they hold as collateral. Indeed, as soon as OCIP failed to meet its margin calls, a brokerage firm, Crédit Suisse First Boston, acted expeditiously to liquidate the collateral it held from Orange County. This first "run on the fund" led to the December bankruptcy.

5

Damned Derivatives?

· ·

"Orange County's fatal error: Speculation in derivatives."
NEW YORK TIMES EDITORIAL, DECEMBER 15, 1994

· ·

As soon as the $1.5 billion dollar "paper" loss was announced by Orange County, pundits blamed derivatives once again. It seems that derivatives have been referred to as "any financial transaction in which a large amount of money is lost." A more scientific definition is that derivatives are assets whose value "derives" from that of some underlying asset. The return on a derivative product is linked to the performance of the underlying asset, which may be a bond, a currency, a commodity, or a number of other things.

Derivative instruments need not be complicated. When you buy a share of IBM worth $85, you pay immediately in cash. Consider now a *forward contract* (a derivative product) on a share of stock. We will discuss forwards more later, but let us define them now as *a promise to buy an asset at a fixed price at some time in the future.* Say you agree to buy a share of IBM at $85 in six months. If before expiration of the contract, the stock price falls to $80, the contract has lost $5 in value for you. Pretty simple. In fact, the reverse repos entered by Citron can be viewed as forward contracts, because he promised to purchase the securities at a fixed price in the future.

Again, remember that the value of a forward contract *derives* from that of an underlying asset (in our example, a share of stock). And the contract thus becomes an "asset" itself: something capable of being bought and sold.

The Orange County bankruptcy has led to increased scrutiny of derivatives markets. Several companies have suffered dangerously large losses in derivatives in recent years. Since 1987, publicly disclosed derivatives losses in the United States have risen by more than $10 billion. The global derivatives market has been estimated at $35 *trillion* (twelve zeroes). This sum is truly staggering. The total annual Gross National Product for the United States is only $7 trillion, by way of illustration. The total value of global stocks and bonds, for that matter, is only $32 trillion. No wonder the rapid growth in derivatives has sharply focused the attention of regulators and lawmakers.

Derivatives have been portrayed as monster creatures to be feared and chained. No doubt this has to do with the sheer volume of trading in derivatives, but it also reflects a mystique of complexity and danger attached to them.

There are well over a hundred varieties of derivatives, many with perplexing names. Some of these are *caps, diffs, floors, swaptions, inverse floaters, knock-outs, step-ups,* and *binaries.* Without a doubt, the advent of computers and modern microelectronics has allowed for the creation of some highly sophisticated financial instruments—many of them cooked up by mathematicians and even physicists.

In their purest form, derivatives include *forward contracts, futures, swaps,* and *options,* which we will define shortly. They are also hidden in mortgages and in debt instruments called *structured notes.* Our purpose is to provide an intuitive understanding of derivatives, not just because this helps explain the Orange County experience, but because derivatives increasingly permeate pension and mutual funds. The ordinary investor is likely to be "involved" with derivatives whether knowing it or not.

One approach to derivatives is simply to ignore them. Unfortunately, this does not work. Companies have been sued for *not* using derivatives. In 1992, for instance, an Indiana grain coop suffered losses when grain prices fell. The directors were sued and found liable for retaining a manager inexperienced in derivatives.

Types of Derivatives

Most derivatives are *private contracts*. Unlike shares of stock, which are issued by a company and purchased by investors, derivative contracts are created out of "thin air" and represent private agreements between buyers and sellers, defining rules about how the contract value will evolve over time. Thus, a derivative contract is a zero-sum game. Every dollar (or billion) lost by one party is gained by the other.

Derivatives can be traded either over a decentralized network of banks, which is called the *over-the-counter* (OTC) *market,* or on *organized exchanges,* with an actual physical location where all trades occur. For instance, interest-rate derivatives are traded actively on the Chicago Board of Trade. Exchanges are accessible to individual investors through any broker. The OTC market includes all major commercial and investment banks and is accessible only to corporations or large investors.

1. Forward contracts. These are agreements to exchange a given asset at a fixed time in the future. The contract specifies the quantity, date, and price at which the exchange will be transacted.

A forward contract can be used to lock in a price in the future. A U.S. exporter to Germany, for instance, might have agreed to take payment in Deutsche marks (DM) for a shipment of goods in six months. Until that time, the exporter is exposed to the risk of a fall in the dollar value of the DM, which would lead to a decrease in his or her dollar revenues. To avoid this possibility, the exporter calls up a bank and enters a *forward sale* of DM for dollars, agreeing to provide X number of DM for Y number of dollars. Thus one locks in the current rate of exchange. The exporter is *hedged* against movements in the rate of exchange over the next few months and presumably sleeps better at night.

Forward contracts are typically traded OTC; they are tailored to the needs of the client (e.g., in terms of dollar amount and date) and are generally held until expiration.

2. Futures contracts. These are akin to forward contracts but are standardized, negotiable, and traded on organized exchanges. Unlike forwards, which are tailored to customers' needs, futures have a limited choice of expiration dates and trade in fixed contract sizes. This standardization ensures easy trading and an active market. Otherwise, futures are very similar to forwards (e.g., in terms of pricing). Because they are traded on organized exchanges they can be traded by individual investors.

3. Swaps. These are agreements between two parties to exchange a series of cash flows in the future according to a formula. Returning to our example, the U.S. exporter might arrange to pay a fixed amount in DM every six months for the next five years in return for a fixed stream of receipts in dollars. Swaps are typically traded OTC. (The Orange County fund invested in structured notes whose payoffs were tied to swap rates.)

4. Options. These are instruments that give their holder the right to buy or sell an asset at a specified (delivery) price until a specified expiration date. Options to buy are *call op-*

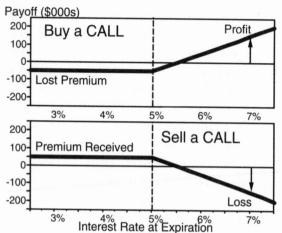

Payoff ($000s)

Figure 5.1. Payoff on a Call Option

tions; options to sell are *put options*. As options confer a right, but not an obligation, they will be exercised only if they generate profits; in contrast, forwards involve an obligation to either buy or sell and can generate profits or losses. Options are traded both on exchanges and OTC.

Options are fundamental instruments, the "quarks" of finance. They can serve as building blocks for nearly any financial contract. Options are also important because they appear, or hide, in many common assets such as mortgages and structured notes.

To see how an option works, consider an option to buy one share of IBM, which trades at $85, with a delivery price of $90 in six months. If IBM stays at $85, the holder of the call will not exercise, since the price is less than $90 and the option is not profitable. However, if IBM goes to $100, the holder will exercise the right to buy at $90 and will acquire the stock, now worth $100, for a profit of $10. More generally, instead of actually buying an asset, it is sufficient simply to define a payoff at expiration. For instance, the contract may specify a payoff to the buyer of $10 if IBM trades at $100, $15 if at $105, and so on.

Because options generate profits at expiration (and are abandoned if there are no profits), an option contract is a valuable asset. Therefore, sellers of options require a payment to secure the option contract. This up-front payment, as in insurance, is called a *premium*.

As another example, consider a call option on a short-term interest rate. (Many of these were hidden in securities purchased by the OCIP.) Say the rate is currently 4%. The option contract is written to specify that the buyer will receive $100,000 times the number of percentage points by which interest rates are above 5%. If rates go to 7%, the buyer receives $100,000 x $(7 - 5) = $200,000$. This amount is paid by the option seller. But if rates stay at 4%, the buyer will not exercise the option, which then dies.

To enter such a contract, the buyer pays the *option premium*. Let us say the market determines that the fair value of such a premium—a right to take profits but not suffer losses— is $50,000. This is a "sunk" cost, that is, payable whatever happens later.

Figure 5.1 displays the payoff at expiration from a call option on an interest rate. The horizontal axis in Figure 5.1 represents the future value of interest rates; the vertical axis the dollar payoff at expiration. The top panel shows the payoff from buying a call option, the bottom panel the payoff from selling a call option. The buyer of the option is said to be "long," the seller is "short."

Clearly, if rates stay at 5% or move lower, the cost to the buyer of the option will be the (future) value of $50,000. Only if rates go up does he or she make a profit. Note also that for any interest rate, the sum of payoffs from the "long" and the "short" is zero.

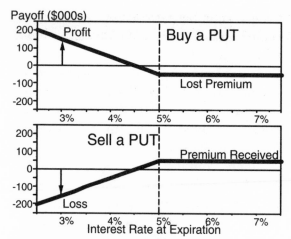

Figure 5.2. Payoff on a Put Option

Figure 5.2 displays the payoff at expiration from a put option on an interest rate. Here, the large profits or losses occur for falling rates. As before, gains and losses sum to zero.

A *cap* is a call option on interest rates. An interest rate *floor* is a put option, which pays off if rates fall. A rate *collar* is a combination of a cap and a floor.

These graphs suggest why investors can lose large amounts of money in options trading. Selling options can be dangerous: it is much like selling insurance. The seller collects a premium, which can be very profitable, unless and until a large movement occurs. Such a movement can lead to catastrophe.

Selling options, however, is particularly appealing to investors who seek high yields. When interest rates are low, as in 1993 (3–4%), it becomes tempting to supercharge a portfolio by selling options. A broker, for instance, may call up and describe a "safe" investment with an attractive 6% yield. The problem is that the extra 2 or 3% over the market rate represents the premium received from selling an option.

Table 5.1.

Major Derivatives Markets

| Instrument | Exchanges | Over-the-Counter | | |
	Futures, Options	Forwards, Options, Swaps	Structured Notes	Mortgage Derivatives
Market size (billion)	$10,700	$24,400	$250	$710
Type	Contracts	Contracts	Securities	Securities
Choices	Limited	Unlimited	Unlimited	Narrow
Liquidity	Very liquid	Liquid	Illiquid	Illiquid
Pricing	Simple	Simple	Difficult	Hellish
Default risk	About none	Some	Some	About none
Market structure	Very competitive	Some competition	Not competitive	Some competition

Everything will be fine unless the underlying financial variable sustains a large movement in the wrong direction. Then an investor can lose 10–50% of his or her capital. This explains why many municipalities have been burned by investing in bonds such as collateralized mortgage obligations (CMOs) that involve embedded (hidden) *short* positions in options.

The problem lies not with the instrument itself, but with uninformed use of it. If an investor is knowledgeable about the inherent risks—or has in his or her portfolio other assets to offset the potential loss of option value—it may be appropriate to sell options. The question then boils down to price (the option premium). If high enough, it may be worthwhile to collect, because the premium will more than compensate for possible future losses, on average.

Selling options is a delicate art, similar to selling insurance. And some insurance companies do better than others.

An executive of a successful firm once said, "In insurance, there is no bad risk—there are only bad prices [premiums]." Dealing in options involves both art and technique.

One could argue that derivatives are more significant even than this, because they appear in *structured notes* and in some *mortgage-backed securities* as well. (These instruments will be discussed in a following chapter.) Structured notes and mortgages have complex patterns of payoffs; in a way, they stand as hybrids between pure securities and pure derivatives. To summarize, then, Table 5.1 provides a fuller picture of the market for derivatives, with some notes about the characteristics of different instruments.

6

Structured Notes

· · · · · · · · · · · · · · · · · · · ·

Caveat emptor (**buyer beware**).

· ·

Notes are said to be "structured" when their conditions are customized to some buyer's specifications. Robert Citron invested heavily in structured notes ($8 billion worth) on behalf of OCIP. With a structured note, payments do not take the form of a fixed coupon amount; instead, they are indexed to some financial variable, often in creative ways, like derivatives contracts. Market participants estimate that about 30% of the new-issue note volume in 1993 consisted of structured notes.

We will first take a look at a "plain vanilla" structured note product, the floating rate note. Then we will discuss the notorious "inverse floater," which played an important role in the OCIP strategy.

As its name implies, a floating rate note (FRN) is a debt instrument with a variable interest payment. Adjustments are made periodically (often every six months) and are tied to a

Structured Notes

Table 6.1.

Pricing a "Floater" ($100 million indexed to 6-month LIBOR)

Reset Date	LIBOR	Interest Payment
December 1993	3%	
June 1994	5%	$(1/2) \times (3\%) \times \$100m = \$1.5m$
December 1994	7%	$(1/2) \times (5\%) \times \$100m = \$2.5m$
June 1995	6%	$(1/2) \times (7\%) \times \$100m = \$3.5m$

money-market index such as the London interbank offer rate (LIBOR). LIBOR is the cost of funds for large banks in the London market and has become a benchmark rate for short-term capital costs.

Table 6.1 shows how the coupon payment might be set for a $100 million FRN. On December 31, 1993, LIBOR was at 3%. The coupon payment set for six months hence was $(1/2) \times (3\%) \times \$100$ million $= \$1.5$ million (half the annual payment). If after six months, LIBOR had increased to 5%, the coupon payment would have gone up accordingly.

The salient feature of FRNs is that their value does not depend very much on interest rates. The coupon is reset periodically to the current interest rate; if rates go up, the coupon follows, and conversely if rates go down. The market value of the note itself is relatively insensitive to changes in rates.

FRNs are similar to cash. Investing in FRNs thus entails a very low risk of loss of principal. So, the maturity of an FRN is not important; some are even issued as "perpetual" instruments, that is, without a fixed redemption date. From the essence of the FRN, however, was created a monstrous creature: the *inverse floater*.

Table 6.2

Pricing an "Inverse Floater" ($100 million indexed to 8% minus 6-month LIBOR)

Reset Date	LIBOR	Interest Payment
December 1993	3%	
June 1994	5%	$(1/2) \times (8\% - 3\%) \times \$100m = \$2.5m$
December 1994	7%	$(1/2) \times (8\% - 5\%) \times \$100m = \$1.5m$
June 1995	6%	$(1/2) \times (8\% - 7\%) \times \$100m = \$0.5m$

Inverse Floaters

Inverse floater notes make payments that move *inversely* with movements in a benchmark rate. As interest rates go up, the coupon paid declines.

Table 6.2 shows how to compute the coupon for an inverse floater that pays 8% minus LIBOR. The reference rate of 8% is determined by the issuer. As before, assume that in December 1993 LIBOR was at 3%. The coupon payment set for six months was then $(1/2) \times (8\% - 3\%) \times \$100$ million = $2.5 million. If after six months, LIBOR increased to 5%, the coupon payment would have gone down to $1.5 million. If rates went up to 8% or above, the coupon payment would fall to zero. From the viewpoint of the note holder, this is the worst possible outcome, of course.

The OCIP was chock-full of inverse floaters issued by the federal agencies such as "Fannie Mae" (Federal National Mortgage Association). They first appeared in 1986. One motive for issuing such securities is to hedge an exposure to changing interest rates. A thrift institution, for instance, typically borrows funds from depositors at a rate that can change but invests in mortgages with fixed rates. These assets and liabilities are mismatched in the sense that an increase in interest rates will squeeze the institution between higher cost of funds (interest paid to depositors) and fixed revenues (from mortgage payments). This mismatch can be offset by issuing an inverse floater, because the increase in interest rates will lower capital costs to the issuer.

Inverse floaters are complicated to price. Their fair market value can be found by constructing a portfolio of assets with the same payoffs as the inverse floater. For example,

$100 million Inverse floater 8% − LIBOR		$200 million Fixed rate note 4%		$100 million FRN at LIBOR		$100 million Cap option at 8%
	=		−		+	

In this example, the cap option generates a payment to the holder of the note if LIBOR goes above 8%; it is worth a maximum of (LIBOR − 8%) and zero at each coupon payment. For instance, if LIBOR goes up to 9%, the cap pays $100 million times (9% − 8%). This ensures that the coupon payment does not fall below zero. The opposite of a cap is a "floor" option, which generates a payment if interest rates fall. Caps and floors are essentially impossible to price for unsophisticated investors—banks price them using powerful computers.

The $200 million term in the decomposition shows that *inverse floaters are quite sensitive to movements in interest rates.* The exposure of a 5-year inverse floater is similar to twice that of a straight 5-year fixed-rate note, or about that of a 10-year note. Inverse floaters typically start with high coupons, but they run the risk of sharp price falls if interest rates increase. At a time of rising rates, OCIP was using these instruments to bet on *stable or falling* interest rates (see Box 6.1).

Box 6.1 A Supercharged Inverse Floater

The Orange County Investment Pool invested $100 million in a structured note issued by the Federal Home Loan Board (FHLB) that pays 15.5% minus twice the LIBOR rate. From January 1993 to November 1994, LIBOR went up sharply, leading to a fall in the coupon paid:

Date	LIBOR	Coupon payment
January 1993	3.625%	8.25%
November 1994	6.50%	2.50%

Because the note is indexed to twice the LIBOR rate, the note is equivalent to 3 conventional fixed-rate notes minus 2 FRNs plus some options. Its exposure is about *three* times that of a conventional fixed-rate note with the same maturity.

As we have seen, from the viewpoint of the issuer, a structured note can be an especially convenient way to raise capital. Issuing a structured note may allow an issuer to share the business risks with a buyer. From the viewpoint of the buyer (investor), structured notes permit speculation on a broad range of prices and variables, often in conveniently specific ways. For instance, a structured note may contain a long-term (e.g., 5-year) currency option, something not easy to find in other markets. As with other instruments, structured notes permit speculators to put into play their best guesses about aspects of financial reality. But convenience and specificity come at a cost: these notes are often devilish to price adequately, which is why we need to turn to "rocket scientists."

7

Rocket Scientists—
It Gets Technical

· ·

Per ardua ad astra (**through difficulties to the stars**).

· ·

Robert Citron used structured notes to implement a particular view on interest rates. (As it turned out, a seriously incorrect view.) But any investor who ventures into the world of "inverse floaters" and the like must sooner or later grapple with the problem of how to determine their fair market value.

An inverse floater can be priced as described in Box 7.1. This example gives a good idea of the level of complexity of the problem. This equation is typical of those to be solved for finding the price of a derivative product. To the untrained eye, the problem appears hellish, but readers with a background in advanced mathematics or physics will recognize a familiar creature: the partial differential equation. Such equations are common in engineering, where they are used for, among other things, building rockets. Modern financial engineers are, in consequence, referred to sometimes as *rocket scientists.* For instance, Scott Peng, the author of a book on structure notes, has a Ph.D. in applied plasma physics from MIT.

Box 7.1. Valuing an Inverse Floater

First, assume a mean-reverting process for the interest rate r, whose movement dr can be characterized as

$$dr = k(\theta - r)dt + \sigma \sqrt{r}\, dz,$$

where dt is the time increment, θ the long-run value of r, $k<1$ is the speed of mean-reversion toward the long-run value, σ is the volatility of interest rates, and dz is a random component. Now, we are trying to value a (derivative) security whose value P depends *only* on r and time t. P can be found by solving the partial differential equation,

$$(1/2)\, \sigma^2 r^2\, P_{rr} + [k(\theta - r) - \lambda\, r]P_r + P_t + c(r,t) - rP = 0.$$

We seek to find a function P (not a number), that is such that its first-order derivatives with respect to time and r, P_t and P_r, as well as its second-order derivative P_{rr}, satisfy this relationship, subject to appropriate boundary conditions. One such condition is that the price must converge to the face value at expiration. For an inverse floater, the coupon payment $c(r,t)$ is defined as a fixed rate R minus the current rate r, if positive. Et voilà!

In the past 20 years, the pricing of derivative and fixed-income products has become quite sophisticated. Louis Bachelier, a French mathematician, offered the first option pricing model in 1900. Paul Samuelson introduced important improvements in the late 1960s, but Samuelson's approach involved the use of unknown parameters, which made it less practicable than it might have been. A major breakthrough came in the early 1970s. Fisher Black and Myron Scholes, of the University of Chicago, devised a rigorous yet flexible method for pricing options (the equation in Box 7.1). This Black–Scholes creation has been described as "the most successful model in applied economics." The closed-form solution to the equation is by now familiar to all option traders.

Dynamic Hedging

The Black–Scholes approach incorporates an important insight: trading in options can be replicated by "dynamic hedging." For our purposes, *dynamic hedging* can be defined as "trading in the underlying asset of an option, for the purpose of duplicating the pattern of payoffs of the option."

In our attempt to replicate a call option, we start with 50% cash and 50% invested in the asset. As the asset price increases, we progressively purchase more of the asset until we are fully invested at expiration. The position is similar to that of a call option at expiration, where the holder of the call exercises the option and buys the asset. Note also that one buys more of the asset *after* its price has gone up; so, this pattern of trading creates costs, through systematic buying at higher prices, that replicate the sunk cost of the option premium.

In short, there is an equivalence between holding an option and a particular pattern of trading in an asset. Furthermore, even when an asset contains no option, an option-*like* payoff can be created by active buying and selling.

This equivalence was nowhere more apparent than in the transactions of OCIP under Robert Citron. The portfolio was composed of bonds, which fall in price as interest rates increase. As interest rates rose, Bob Citron attempted to cover losses by *increasing* his exposure to interest rate risk; that is, buying additional bonds or longer duration instruments or adding on repos, as the bond market tanked.

But buying more of an instrument when its price falls is exactly opposite to the pattern given previously (which we have seen is equivalent to buying a call option). Citron was implementing a dynamic trading strategy, all right, but it was equivalent to *selling* a call option on interest rates. And such a strategy is totally inconsistent with the goal of preserving capital.

Financial Engineers

The Black–Scholes model is useful for pricing "plain vanilla" options. For other derivative products, however, the solution to the equation can be found only through numerical simulations performed on computers.

A new industry has emerged—that of "financial engineering"—devoted to the rigorous study of hybrid financial securities. Financial engineers are now essential elements in the risk management system of any financial institution. Routinely, they use powerful workstations to price derivatives. Evaluating mortgages, in particular, requires very fast machines, especially when assets need to be priced many times over the course of a trading day. Citibank, for instance, recently purchased a Cray 6400 supercomputer to price mortgage securities more quickly. Robert Citron neither used such machines nor does he seem to have been aware of their importance.

With advanced computing power, financial engineers have created some truly exotic derivative products. The downside of this burst of creativity, which has brought investors knock-out options, barrier options, as-you-like-it options, and binary options, not to mention ARPs, CATs, ICONs, LYONs, SPINs, and ZEBRAs, is that unwary investors may be offered products they are helpless to evaluate. Furthermore, derivatives traded on the OTC market, being highly unusual or tailor-made, cannot be easily compared for purposes of pricing (because investors cannot shop around to get a quote from another bank).

Box 7.2. Is Derivatives Talk Greek to You?

If you were to listen to a conversation between derivatives traders, it would probably sound Greek to you. Rocket scientists have developed their own technical jargon. Part of this nerdy game is to come up with new zippy names for fancy products based on Greek letters. Here is a sample of commonly used terms:

α (alpha) measure of abnormal performance
β (beta) how a particular stock reacts to movements in the stock market
γ (gamma) how the delta changes
δ (delta) how a derivative reacts to the price of the underlying variable
ε (epsilon) the unexplained, or error, term
θ (theta) the effect of the passage of time on a derivative
λ (lambda) how a derivative reacts to changes in the volatility
μ (mu) the expected return on an asset
ρ (rho) a measure of the closeness of movements between the prices of two assets
σ (sigma) the volatility, or possible range, of values for price movements
ϕ (phi) the standard normal distribution function (bell curve).

Note that some letters, such as zeta and xi are carefully avoided because difficult to write. After all, financial engineers are not artists. Soon, they will run out of the 24-letter alphabet and maybe move to cyrillic.

The best advice may be this: treat exotic derivatives like powerful medicines, large doses of which can be harmful. Use them in moderation, for a particular purpose (such as risk management) and only after having read the instructions on the bottle.

In case of doubt about derivatives, it is better to ask the opinion of experts. The recent publicity about derivatives has led many corporations and investors to seek a new kind of advice about risk.

Newly created consulting firms, such as New York's Capital Market Risk Advisors (CMRA), are filling a niche created by the anxiety surrounding derivatives (and other financial issues). CMRA played an important role in the Orange County crisis: Orange County officials, acting over Robert Citron's head, turned to CMRA in October 1994, seeking an objective reading on OCIP's position. CMRA had the help of TSA Capital Management, a Los Angeles bond firm that specializes in exotic securities. TSA provided the first objective analysis of the many structured notes held by the county. Organizations like CMRA evaluate portfolios, test the validity of financial strategies, and even assess the technology and software in use. They speak from a disinterested position: unlike banks or brokers, their concern is not to sell financial products to an investor.

8

The Need for Capital

· ·

Pecuniae obediunt omnia (**money makes the world go round**).

· ·

I t is now time to take a closer look at the composition of Citron's pool. Just before the bankruptcy, the OCIP had invested $310 million in Treasury securities (issued by the federal government), $14,100 million in agency securities, $170 million in mortgage-backed securities (MBSs), and $2,800 million in corporate debt. Each of these will be examined in this chapter. OCIP also incurred debt (that is, raised funds) by issuing municipal bonds of its own. Chapter 12 deals with the municipal market.

Table 8.1 provides a breakdown of the U.S. public bond market. As of December 1993, this market amounted to about $6.9 trillion. Citron's portfolio made him one of the "largest investors in the U.S.," as he once bragged. His agency portfolio was worth $14 billion, which is equivalent to 2.6% of the conventional agency market. This is enormous for a single investor.

One attractive feature of government and agency securities is that their credit risk, or risk of default, is viewed as

Table 8.1

The U.S. Bond Market—Total Outstanding Public Bonds, 1993 ($ billion)

Federal Government	2,275
Federal Agencies:	
Mortgage backed	1,350
Conventional	549
Nonagency mortgage backed	250
Municipals	988
Corporate	1,455
Total	6,867

Source: Salomon Brothers, "How Big Is the World Bond Market?" Bonds include only issues with a maturity beyond one year.

very low. This was also true of the municipal bond sector; that is, until the Orange County default. Low credit risk is why public investment pools, much concerned with the safety of their investments, make heavy use of government securities. However, *safety of principal does not mean freedom from risk*. Indeed, such securities can be heavily exposed to interest rate change, sometimes in ways difficult to gauge.

Treasury Securities

Treasury securities are direct obligations of the federal government. They are issued by the U.S. Treasury in what is called the *primary* market, to raise funds for the government; for example, they are used to finance the budget deficit. As we see from Table 8.1, the federal government had $2,275 billion of notes and bonds outstanding at the end of 1993. This represented about half of the total federal debt ($4,562 billion as of December 1993).

Table 8.2

Outstanding Agency Debt ($ billion)

	Dec. 1991	Dec. 1993	June 1994
Federally Related Agencies	36	41	43
Federally Sponsored Agencies:	375	402	604
Federal Farm Credit Bank	55	52	54
Farm Credit Financial Assistance Corp.	1	1	1
Federal National Mortgage Association	116	134	228
Federal Home Loan Banks	136	108	161
Federal Home Loan Mortgage Corp.	26	30	73
Financing Corp.	8	8	8
Resolution Trust Corp.	5	30	30
Student Loan Marketing Association	29	38	48
Total	412	443	647

Source: Federal Reserve *Bulletin*.

Treasury securities are generally not redeemable prior to maturity. They can, however, be sold in the *secondary* market, which is an extremely active over-the-counter market. In 1994, the average daily volume of trading in Treasuries was $170 billion. Treasury securities, because of their good liquidity and low default risk, are benchmarks of values in the fixed-income sector. For instance, the "long bond," which is the most recently issued 30-year bond, is widely watched as a barometer of interest rates.

The Agency Market

Most of the bonds held by OCIP were issued by federal agencies in need of capital. These agencies, federally sponsored or guaranteed, were created by Congress to reduce the costs of capital for selected sectors of the economy. Because the market perceives that the government will not allow these agencies to default, agency securities are considered the closest to government debt in terms of credit risk. Again, although the risk of default is very low, agency securities do involve interest rate risk.

These agencies can be broadly classified into federally related agencies and federally sponsored agencies. The first category consists of entities of the government that borrow through the *Federal Financing Bank.* They include, among others, the Export-Import Bank, the Government National Mortgage Association, the Small Business Administration, and the Tennessee Valley Authority. As of 1993, their cumulative outstanding debt was $41 billion.

Federally sponsored agencies require much more capital. Table 8.2 shows the total amount of debt issued by all agencies. There are currently eight of them:

- The *Federal Farm Credit Bank* and *Farm Credit Financial Assistance Corporation* provide loans to the agricultural sector.
- The *Federal National Mortgage Association* (FNMA, or "Fannie Mae"), the *Federal Home Loan Bank* (FHLB), and the *Federal Home Loan Mortgage Corporation* ("Freddie Mac") provide credit to the housing sector.
- The *Financing Corporation* and the *Resolution Trust Corporation* were created to deal with the bailout of the savings and loan industry.
- The *Student Loan Marketing Association* ("Sallie Mae") provides funds to students for higher education.

These federally sponsored agencies sell notes and bonds of various maturities and, as of June 1994, had accumulated a total debt of $604 billion. Agencies aggressively enter the fixed-income market to raise capital at the cheapest possible cost, sometimes at a risk to taxpayer-investors (remember the dangers of pricing structured notes).

Agency debt is not formally guaranteed by the federal government, and as such, is subject to *credit risk.* To compensate for the risk of default by the issuing agency, agency securities generally trade at higher yields, or lower prices, than federal debt of equivalent maturity. Take for instance two notes identical but for the issuer, the Fannie Mae note expiring in June 1998 (coupon of 5.38%) and the Treasury note of June 1998 (coupon of 5.25%). Before the Orange County crisis, the Treasury issue sold at a yield of 7.54% and the FNMA issue at 7.72%; the difference in yields, called the *yield spread,* reflected investors' demands for higher returns from an FNMA issue.

Yield spreads can vary over time to reflect the changing financial fortunes of different agencies, but they are generally rather stable. Assuming there is little risk of default by agencies, investing in this kind of debt is a perfectly reasonable way to generate greater income as compared to government debt.

The Mortgage Market

OCIP also held some *mortgage-backed securities.* The sheer size of the MBS market, second only to the federal debt, makes it important to describe. Mortgages are loans undertaken to purchase real estate. Like a repurchase agreement (which, as you will recall, is a loan collateralized by a security), a mortgage is a loan collateralized by a house.

From the point of view of a lending institution, fixed-rate mortgages involve interest rate risk. Typically, a funding institution (such as a savings and loan) will fund itself with short-term deposits, then invest in long-term mortgages. But as we have seen before, this is a recipe for disaster if interest rates go up (remember the "squeeze" between higher rates for depositors and fixed lower rates for mortgages).

Learning from the S&L disaster of the 1980s, lending institutions now unload their mortgages by packaging them and reselling them to other investors. *Mortgage pass-through* securities are created by bundling mortgages into a pool, then offering different interest payoffs to different investors. (*Pass-through* refers to the fact that payments are passed on to investors as mortgage payments come in.) This process of creating tradable securities is called *securitization*.

Since their introduction in 1975, mortgage pass-throughs have grown to more than $1,600 billion. They now account for a third of the U.S. residential mortgage market. Pass-throughs can be issued by private corporations (e.g. thrifts or commercial banks) or by agencies. Government National Mortgage Association (GNMA), FNMA, and Freddie Mac provide guarantees on the timely payment of interest and principal by home buyers. Securities with such guarantees are called *mortgage-backed* securities. The securitization of mortgages has benefited homeowners; some observers estimate that MBSs have lowered the cost of issuing mortgages by 0.25%.

Mortgages, however, have interesting characteristics. Someone taking out a mortgage can *prepay* the loan, for example, when selling the home following a job change or a divorce, say. Also, if interest rates decline, the borrower can refinance at a lower rate without penalty. A homeowner who took on a fixed-rate loan at 12% five years ago would rationally have refinanced in 1993, when mortgage costs fell as low as 7%.

You may recognize in this arrangement a type of derivative instrument—the *option*. This *prepayment option* is favorable to the homeowner, who has purchased and therefore is "long" this option. The holder of the bond is, therefore, "short" the option. As there is no such thing as a free lunch, the borrower must pay a price (for example, through higher-than-regular mortgage payments). Conversely, an investor in mortgage-backed securities should beware of funds offering unusually high yields: they may include the sale of imbedded options. The higher current yield could simply reflect the receipt of the option premium, and the possibility of a capital loss should the option be exercised (as in Figures 5.1 and 5.2). Many of the $14 billion worth of conventional fixed-rate agency notes held by the OCIP were also *callable* by the issuer, which involves the sale of options.

More recently, the mortgage market has evolved into ever-more sophisticated instruments, which have become very complicated to value. Over the last two years, a number of investors have suffered large losses from holding mortgage derivatives such as *collateralized mortgage obligations* (some of which are called *toxic waste*) because they failed to understand the downside potential of selling options. These losses have hit conservative investors such as municipalities and city colleges. But sometimes even sophisticated investors get caught. For example, in April 1987, the brokerage house Merrill Lynch reported a $250 million loss due to mortgage securities trading.

The Corporate Market

Finally, Orange County's funds were also invested in corporate bonds and certificates of deposits (CDs). As the name implies, these are securities issued by corporations to finance investment projects. Corporate debt is subject to interest rate risk as well as the credit risk of the issuer. The OCIP was restricted to invest in issues with low credit risk.

Creditworthiness is assessed by ratings services. Standard & Poor's Ratings Group and Moody's Investors Services regularly assign credit rating to bond issues. Table 8.3 explains the meaning of the ratings.

Table 8.3

Credit Ratings

Explanation	Standard & Poor's	Moody's Services
Highest grade	AAA	Aaa
High grade	AA	Aa
Upper medium grade	A	A
Medium grade	BBB	Baa
Lower medium grade	BB	Ba
Speculative	B	B
Poor quality	CCC	Caa
Highest speculation	CC	Ca
Lowest quality	C	C
In default, rating indicates salvage value	DDD–D	

Using the S&P classification system, securities rated BBB or above are considered *investment grade*; lower rated bonds are given the derogatory—perhaps unjustified—name of *junk bonds*. More properly defined as *high-yield bonds*, junk bonds are issued by firms whose ability to repay depends on their immediate financial fortunes.

Michael Milken, of Drexel Burnham Lambert, initiated this sector of the corporate bond market. He was convicted of securities fraud in 1990. But the high-yield securities market serves an important financial function: it gives small firms access to capital that might otherwise be impossible to acquire. Corporate giants such as MCI Communications first raised funds through debt issues that seemed highly questionable at the time. (MCI is now the 50th largest U.S. corporation in terms of market value, with annual sales of $15 billion.)

To offset credit risk, corporate bond investors require higher yields. Again, receiving this higher yield is similar to selling an option. It puts the principal in jeopardy. The question is whether the high yield compensates for possible future losses.

By now, we have completed our tour of the financial markets. With a necessary understanding of the financial instruments that caused the Orange County fiasco, we can return to our main story.

9

Going Bankrupt
· · · · · · · · · · · · · · · · · ·

"Question #7: How does he fund margin calls?"
ASKED TO THE CITY OF IRVINE, CALIFORNIA, WHICH BOR-
ROWED $62 MILLION TO INVEST IN THE OCIP, APRIL 11, 1994
· ·

A s interest rates threatened to rise further in the fall
of 1994, Matthew Raabe, Orange County assistant
treasurer, became more and more concerned about
OCIP's position. All during the election campaign of the previous spring, Raabe had worked loyally for his boss, articulat-
ing Robert Citron's investment strategy when Citron himself
was at a loss for words. Raabe, who had worked in the Treasurer's office since 1987, had a gift for simplifying complex
issues. Participants in the pool, such as city governments and
school districts, having been disturbed by John Moorlach's
sharp attacks on Citron, found Raabe's explanations sooth-
ing and much more intelligible than Citron's own.

But Raabe, aware that the county's portfolio was steadily losing value, finally stopped believing his own reassur-
ances. On October 24, he approached Ernie Schneider, the

county's chief administrative officer, and Steve Lewis, auditor-controller, to express his concern. "All through July, August, September," Raabe has recalled, "there was over a billion dollars in available cash . . . so everything looked really good. But the end of October report showed that the available cash was dwindling. . . . It went down from $1 billion, my recollection is, to $450 million."

Alerted by Raabe, the county hired Capital Market Risk Advisers, at a fee of $300,000, to assess the county portfolio. Still, Raabe was only vaguely aware of the extent of OCIP's peril: "Even at the time I made my concerns known, I mentioned that there was a good chance I was overreacting to the situation," Raabe says. "I said I hoped it would prove out that I just made an embarrassing mistake."

But Raabe's instincts were correct. Over the next few weeks he provided CMRA with hundreds of documents, and the analysts began to form an impression of a badly mismanaged fund. "They were surprised that for a portfolio of that size," Raabe recalls, "with the reputation it had, it was really unsophisticated." Finally, on November 16, CMRA presented a preliminary report to county officials. The pool had suffered a severe loss, they found, amounting to $1.5 billion or more. There were major cash-flow problems, and the county might be unable to meet millions in interest payments that would soon come due. This news, which affected Raabe, as he says, "like I was punched in the stomach," was not the final verdict, however. CMRA needed more time to evaluate all the securities held by the pool. Though frightening, OCIP's losses were only on "paper" so far, and if a run of investors did not develop and if interest rates remained as they were, OCIP might yet reorganize and right itself.

In particular, property tax payments were coming due December 10. These checks, to be written to Robert L. "Bob" Citron could help the OCIP ride out its liquidity problems.

Raabe, 38 years old at the time, studied business administration at Cal. State, Fullerton. A certified public accountant, he learned about municipal investing during his service in the Treasurer's office, and he would later claim to have been very much a junior partner to Citron. "I assumed he knew what he was doing," he said about Citron's management of the OCIP; and at state senate hearings in January 1995, he claimed never to have had a clear understanding of the workings of the fund.

Still, Raabe often met with contributors, persuading them that their principal was not at risk and on occasion even inducing them to increase their level of investment. For example, in 1993 he oversaw an agreement whereby four school districts actually *borrowed* funds ($200 million in taxable notes) to invest in OCIP.

The *Orange County Register,* in an editorial published after the bankruptcy, described investors' feelings toward Raabe by naming him the "deputy of deception." Yet he was the first to blow the whistle, and played a prominent and difficult role, mediating between CMRA and the county and quietly working around Citron, who by most accounts was woefully out of touch. Even after CMRA had delivered its preliminary report in November, "[Citron] felt strongly that his investment strategy was correct," Raabe has said, "that the market was going to turn around and he was going to really have a good year of performance."

An informal "crisis management team" took shape, composed of high county officials (but not the elective Board of Supervisors, who were pointedly kept out of the loop). Raabe continued funneling documents to CMRA via fax and e-mail, and the crisis team prepared for the inevitable confrontation with investors and commercial lenders. Following the 0.75% interest rate increase of November 15, one of these major investors, the Irvine Ranch Water District, headed by Peer Swan, asked to redeem $100 million of the

$400 million it had in OCIP. This request precipitated a general scrutiny of the fund's cash position, and at long last the Board of Supervisors became involved in the crisis.

On November 29, Raabe urged the 10 largest investors not to start a run on the pool. "Whose idea it was I just don't recall," he has said, "but we developed the idea that since a $1.5 billion paper loss translated to a roughly 20% loss if we had to liquidate, anybody who wanted to leave the portfolio would have to accept that 20% market-value loss because it wouldn't be fair for everybody else to pull out and leave the schools and the county holding the bag."

The investors held fast, at least temporarily, and over the next two days (November 30–December 1) Raabe and others communicated by conference calls with Wall Street, hoping to convince the brokers who held the county's collateral that the crisis could be weathered. For the time being, this seemed successful: Wall Street agreed to maintain the county's lines of credit. Then, on December 1, Raabe conducted a press conference, at which Orange County formally announced its $1.5 billion dollar loss. Robert Citron sat dejectedly behind his assistant throughout; it was clear that he had been superseded. The crisis, as serious and shocking as it was, appeared to be lessening.

That Saturday, December 3, the management team met for dinner at Prego, an upscale Italian bistro in Irvine. With much important business to be conducted, again the county Supervisors were excluded: the guest list included only Raabe, Schneider, Lewis, three other top county staffers, and two outside bond counsel. Meanwhile, the stalwart East Coast sources of credit were beginning to grow uneasy. In particular, Crédit Suisse First Boston (CSFB), which held a note for $110 million issued by the county, exercised its seven-day "put" option (declaring its intent to sell the note back in seven days) at the request of investors. OCIP at that time had only $100 million on hand. Furthermore, CSFB decided to call in loans of $1.2 billion from the county, due December 6. CSFB had lent $2.6 billion to OCIP through repos and was the largest such lender. This was the beginning of a wholesale move by commercial lenders to liquidate their Orange County collateral.

Just before the dinner at Prego, Jean Costanza, one of the bond counsel, answered a phone call from CMRA. The news was very bad: Wall Street was starting to panic, and all indications were that lenders would start selling off their collateral on Monday, two days away. The mood of guarded relief at a lessening of the crisis gave way to something more realistic: desperation, depression. By the time the food came, most had lost their appetite. No one ordered dessert. As if unable to grapple with the enormity of the situation, Raabe and the others returned to Raabe's office, and here they took a symbolic step that, although not legally required at the moment, was probably psychologically essential. They researched California law, finding that accusations of impropriety are sufficient grounds for suspension; and they drafted a letter of resignation in which, on the following morning (Sunday, December 4), they strongly urged Robert Citron to sign.

The question now was not whether there would be a disaster: rather, it was how large that disaster would be, and how permanently damaging.

Orange County now faced a simple but unpleasant choice: either reorganize OCIP's holdings, or declare bankruptcy. Because the long-term consequences of bankruptcy were unsettling to contemplate, the county decision makers first explored their other option.

Already, on December 2, CMRA's consultants had been in touch with several Wall Street firms, among them Goldman Sachs, J.P. Morgan, Salomon Brothers, and Swiss Bank Corp. The county hoped that one or another might agree to buy out OCIP's portfolio. To avoid tipping off the markets, these negotiations had to be conducted in secrecy: Orange County was to be known as "Oscar," and the banks just listed were "Golf," "Joe," "Sierra," and "White Cross," respectively. On Saturday morning, CMRA met with bankers in a suite at the Regency Hotel in New York and sifted through the fund's financial data. At a 4 A.M. meeting the following day, the Morgan bankers made a serious offer: they would buy out the fund's unencumbered structured notes for cash. (This $4.4 billion outlay would lead to a profit of about $100 million for "Joe.") A CMRA principal, Tanya Styblo Beder, immediately caught a plane for California to present the Morgan offer to the Supervisors.

The rest of Wall Street, which had hoped to avoid putting a squeeze on the county, nevertheless grew increasingly edgy, especially when news arrived that Robert Citron had resigned. Whether justified or not, his reputation as a "mastermind" still carried weight; now he had been replaced by 38-year-old Matt Raabe, an untested quantity. (Citron later claimed in testimony before the state senate that "if I was still there at that time . . . dealers would not have sold the securities.") There were also rumors on the Street that losses were in fact closer to $3 billion: one expert described the initial loss estimate as "ludicrous."

And the attempt to put the Morgan offer before the Board of Supervisors foundered on an unexpected obstacle: the state "sunshine laws," which require a 24-hour advance notice for public meetings among elected officials. For two days, analysts ran from office to office in the Hall of Administration, trying to explain their plan to the individual Supervisors, each of whom had to be sequestered in a different room.

To satisfy the sunshine laws, the board could not meet before Monday afternoon. Raabe's recommendation was to accept Morgan's offer. There was a problem, however. The fiduciary for the fund, Bob Citron, had just resigned (he had a special responsibility for the funds entrusted to him). None of the Wall Street firms would be willing to take over the securities without a fiduciary.

Then Terry Andrus, the county attorney, raised objections to the plan, as did the law firm of LeBoeuf, Lamb, Greene & MacRae, the outside bond counsel. They argued that the legal status of the fund was so muddled that no one knew who owned which securities. Andrus did not want to indemnify the fiduciary over potential lawsuits. Furthermore, the OCIP investors ought to be consulted before the portfolio was liquidated.

The LeBoeuf attorneys, however, may have had reasons of their own for blocking the plan. In the summer, the law firm had cleared a $600 million taxable note issue whose proceeds went into the investment fund. The offering documents did not disclose that the OCIP had already been subject to large margin calls. The fund's collapse could make the firm vulnerable to bondholder lawsuits. It was only later that the law firm admitted a conflict of interest and stopped representing the county. Faced with this conflicting advice, the board did not approve the rescue plan.

Instead, Andrus raised the possibility of bankruptcy. Bankruptcy might forestall liquidation by brokers. This option would also stop lawsuits against the county and create a centralized forum to resolve all competing claims on the pool.

Meanwhile, on December 5, several million dollars worth of interest payments were to come due. Raabe and other officials made desperate appeals to the SEC, to the State Treasurer's office, to California Attorney General Dan Lungren, to Governor Pete Wilson, and to officials in the Clinton administration. All recognized the gravity of the situation, yet all declined to help Orange County with its "liquidity problem." Assisting the county meant taking on financial responsibility for the pool; the cash-strapped state was in no mood for financial handouts, especially to one of its richest counties.

At around 2 P.M. on December 5, Raabe took a phone call from Nomura Securities, a brokerage house and one of the county's creditors. "[Nomura was] telling me that we had defaulted on our payment to them, and they wanted to know if it was a paperwork problem or what," Raabe recalls. "I said no, we are not going to be able to come up with the cash." The Nomura payment was less than $5 million.

The next day, CS First Boston made its formal request for repayment of $1.25 billion in loans. As the county defaulted, the bank started to liquidate its entire position (about $2.6 billion, mostly reverse repurchase agreements). This started a general run, and within 24 hours, all of the county's creditors, with the exception of Merrill Lynch, had sold the collateral they held against loans. Hurriedly taking the step it had most dreaded, Orange County then declared bankruptcy, seeking protection both for itself and for the investment pool.

The financial earthquake in Orange County produced aftershocks going all the way to Texas, where there was a bank run on the Texas Investment Pool (TexPool). On December 9, a *Wall Street Journal* article appeared that claimed the Texas pool was "running some of the same risk as Orange County." (In fact, the unrealized loss in Texas was only $70 million out of a total pool of $3.7 billion, which represents a loss of just 1.9% of assets.)

Orange County's announcement had big effects elsewhere, as well. Prices in the $1 trillion municipal bond market went down a full percent (a loss of value of around $10 billion). Treasury bonds took a hit of 0.40%. Within California, the damage was especially heavy. Prices of some long-term debt, exclusive of that issued by Orange County, dived by 3–4%.

Also in December 1994, another panic, of even greater magnitude, occurred south of the border. Following a mishandled devaluation, the peso plummeted 40%, causing American investors in Mexican stocks to suffer severe losses.

As in Orange County, the crisis was made more dangerous by many investors trying to exit the market at the same time. In February 1995, as the Mexican situation threatened to deteriorate even further, the U.S. government and the International Monetary Fund put together a bailout package worth $40 billion. These guarantees, functioning much like bank insurance, finally stopped the run on the peso.

Had similar guarantees been provided to the OCIP in December, the run and subsequent bankruptcy might well have been avoided.

Simply stated, a *bank run* occurs when depositors try to withdraw their money in a short period of time. Similarly, the OCIP collapse occurred because investors wanted their money back, and they wanted it right now.

Banks are vulnerable to runs because deposits are invested in assets that may be difficult to sell quickly, such as real estate. Thus, there is a *liquidity mismatch* between assets and liabilities. Note that a bank run does not necessarily imply irrational behavior on the part of depositors. They are promised the full face value of their deposits, and they are paid off on a first-come, first-served basis. Bank runs are rational if investors suspect the total liabilities to them exceed the total assets of the bank. In such a situation, the last investor through the exit door will be the one holding an empty bag.

Thus, bank deposits are by their nature potentially destabilizing. If there is a backup source of liquidity, such as Federal Deposit Insurance, bank runs can usually be avoided.

The fear of a run on the pool explains why Raabe and Citron at first tried to calm investors by characterizing the vanished $1.5 billion as a "paper loss." By withdrawing their funds in advance of others, certain investors hoped to avoid participating in the general collapse. Thus, despite Raabe's and Citron's reassurances, there was a mad rush toward the exit when the original loss was announced December 1. The Irvine Ranch Water District, for example, threatened to pull

$300 million, and the city of Irvine immediately put in a request for $25 million. As other investors began pressing the fund, the county, as we have seen, proposed withholding 20% of principal from those who withdrew. But even this penalty was insufficient to discourage those who feared being last out the door.

The county was also being squeezed at the same time from another direction—New York. Only Merrill Lynch, with $2.1 billion in loans to Orange County, refused to cut off credit. Merrill had done a vast amount of business with OCIP in recent years (in the summer of 1993 alone, the fund purchased $2.7 billion worth of inverse floaters through Michael Stamenson, one of Merrill's most aggressive sales representatives). But other investment houses were less closely identified with OCIP's fortunes. As we have seen, they liquidated their positions vis-à-vis Orange County in great (and perhaps reckless) haste.

This liquidation, unlike that of OCIP's contributors, is hard to rationalize. Whereas investors in the fund were exposed to the full face value of their investment—which had already dropped by some 22%—the brokers were exposed to only the *variation* in the value of their collateral. This was much less than the face value of the securities they held. Indeed, to the extent that additional collateral calls, earlier in the year, had covered the fall in the value of those securities, Wall Street's exposure was relatively slight. In fact, Merrill Lynch, by holding on to its securities, suffered no adverse financial effects. After the liquidation, the OCIP received *excess* collateral back from the brokers.

Defining the Bankruptcy

The Bankruptcy Reform Act of 1978 governs the process of bankruptcy under several "chapters." The one relating to municipal bankruptcies is Chapter 9. Under Chapter 9, a municipality submits to a reorganization of its finances, but there is no provision for the liquidation of assets. Obviously, municipalities cannot be sold off like bankrupt corporations. Also, judges cannot substitute for elected officials in making critical decisions about public services and taxes. In the short run, there is also no impact on a municipality's ability to maintain police protection and other essential services.

An important provision under Chapter 9 is the *automatic stay*, under which payments to creditors are halted and secured creditors prevented from seizing their collateral. Holders of general obligation bonds, suppliers, employees owed back wages, and anyone with insurance or liability claims may have to wait months before being paid.

The full legal ramifications of a Chapter 9 filing are still unclear. Many precedents will undoubtedly be established by the Orange County case, which many predict will provide work for lawyers for years to come. (At a hearing on December 14, the courtroom in Orange County was filled beyond capacity, and bankruptcy attorneys were so numerous they had to wear number tags for identification.)

What is known about bankruptcy is mainly its expense. Relations between the municipality and its employees, and between the municipality and its creditors, are seriously disrupted, which sometimes leads to monumental legal fees. In the first six months alone, Orange County prepared itself for bankruptcy-related litigation expenses in the neighborhood of $24 million. These fees are sure to rise inexorably as the county becomes mired in years of litigation. For example, when LTV, a steel company, filed for bankruptcy in 1987, it paid more than $200 million in legal fees over the following seven years.

In addition, municipal bankruptcy leads to sharply lower credit ratings. With a municipality's debt in default, its bonds are rated even lower than "junk" grade. Even after a successful reorganization, investors will lend to a once-bankrupt municipality only if compensated for the greater risk of default by higher rates of interest.

The stigma of bankruptcy may saddle a city or county with higher borrowing costs for a long time. This is why, in previous bankruptcies, a refinancing authority or an oversight committee or a state agency has often stepped in, guaranteeing adequate supplies of revenue. (New York City and Cleveland, Ohio, have both in recent years been bailed out by their respective states.) The state of California, however, declined to provide guarantees for Orange County; California is cash poor, having yet to emerge fully from the recession of the early 1990s, and the Democrat-controlled legislature may well have been unsympathetic toward the "right-wing bastion" of Orange County.

Preparing for Liquidation

To reorganize, the county first obtained an order from the U.S. Bankruptcy Court under Judge John Ryan, authorizing liquidation of its portfolio. As Bruce Bennett, the Orange County bankruptcy lawyer, put it, "[It's] time to close the casino and put the dice away."

Tom Hayes, a former California state treasurer, accepted appointment as the county's financial reorganizer. The county also hired Salomon Brothers to help evaluate and reposition the portfolio.

Hayes had been appointed state treasurer in 1989. During his tenure, he was known for conservatively managing the state's $20 billion portfolio. After two years at the helm, he ran for election to the post, but lost the contest to Kathleen Brown, who criticized him for earning less than the Orange County pool. (Such was Citron's reputation.) After Brown defeated him, Governor Pete Wilson appointed Hayes as California chief financial advisor, a job where he helped to oversee the state's $60 billion budget.

Table 9.1

Portfolio on December 13

	Face Value (billion)	Loss (billion)	Loss (percent of investment)
Amount invested	$7.42		
Reverse repos	$12.64		
Initial portfolio	$20.06		
Collateral sale	$11.00	$1.32	17.8%
Remaining portfolio:	$9.06	$0.70	9.4%
Owed to brokers	$3.10		
To investors	$5.96		
Total		$2.02	27.2%

On December 13, William Rifkin, head of the Salomon team, announced the most detailed estimates yet of the portfolio position. The liquidation of collateralized securities had led to a realized loss of $1.3 billion dollars. The rest of the portfolio had lost $700 million on paper, thus creating an estimated loss of $2.0 billion. The total face value of the portfolio had been reduced to $9 billion, of which some value was due brokers. These losses are detailed in Table 9.1.

Of the remaining portfolio, 60% was in structured notes, up from 47% because of Wall Street's sales of collateral. The structured notes had lost 10.1% of their value, against 4.4% for the conventional securities. (As explained previously, structured notes such as inverse floaters have a duration double that of conventional securities, which doubles the loss.)

Tom Hayes's task was to organize an orderly sale of the 90-some securities in the portfolio. This job would be made more difficult by the specialized features of the $5 billion worth of structured notes. At the time Hayes took control, the fund's interest exposure was such that, for every percentage increase in rates, OCIP stood to lose an additional $300 million. Hayes's options were these:

1. Selling in blocks. This means liquidating piecemeal. Salomon Brothers would announce auctions of securities, which would go to the highest bidder. The main risk of such a strategy is that the sale takes time, during which the portfolio might suffer losses if rates continued to rise.

2. Selling as a single unit. This means finding a single buyer willing to bid for the entire portfolio. Such a strategy avoids market risks because of its speed (at least in theory). The downside is that sale as a single unit brings less favorable prices compared to sale in blocks.

3. Immediate hedging, followed by liquidation over time. This strategy offers protection against further rises in rates. It can be implemented in a number of ways: by selling interest-rate futures contracts, by entering interest-rate forward or swap contracts, or by buying interest-rate options as protection. The drawback of the hedging strategy is that it does not generate cash needed for making immediate payments.

4. Maintaining the portfolio. This means following the investment strategy already in place, specifically, Robert Citron's strategy, which might produce a turnaround if interest rates were to fall. However, this would not have generated cash nor was it politically feasible considering Citron's low esteem. Further, there was a meeting of the Federal Reserve Board looming on December 20. It was widely anticipated that the Fed would raise rates even further.

In the end, Hayes followed the first strategy, that of selling off the portfolio in blocks. This exposed the fund to some

Table 9.2

The Portfolio Liquidation

Type	Face Value	Market Value	Percent Loss
Agencies	3,821	3,517	8.0
Certificates of deposit	1,315	1,171	11.0
Mortgage-backed securities	196	181	7.7
Corporates	1,945	1,788	8.1
Mutual funds	275	252	8.4
Total	7,552	6,909	8.5

market risk, which, as it happened, was beneficial due to a slight decrease in interest rates in the ensuing weeks.

Once the portfolio was sold, the receipts were reinvested in very short-term securities such as Treasury bills. But there were substantial transaction costs. Financial intermediaries buy from a client at a *bid* price, but then sell at a higher *ask* price. The difference, known as the *bid-ask spread*, was at least 0.25% for the securities involved in these transactions. This translated into fees of 0.25% times $7.5 billion, or a $19 million cost for the liquidation of the remaining portfolio.

The restructuring proceeded with dispatch—it took only six weeks to complete. In the end, $7.5 billion of securities were sold, of which $4.7 billion went to the county and the remainder to repay outstanding loans.

Table 9.2 details the various instruments and losses. For agency bonds, MBSs, corporate notes, and mutual funds, the losses were on the order of 8% of principal. The certificates of deposit, many of which were similar to structured notes, lost 11.0% of their value.

The interest rate exposure of the portfolio decreased successively over time. From December 13 to 22, the exposure

Table 9.3

Counting up the Losses ($ billion)

	Initial Dec. 12	Revised Jan. 17
Amount invested	7.42	7.57
Investment portfolio:	5.40	5.88
Securities	5.03	5.16
Cash equivalents	0.23	0.54
Excess collateral	0.14	0.18
Loss:	2.02	1.69
Percent Loss	27.2%	22.3%

went from a $300 million to a $220 million loss for every point increase in rates. A week later, portfolio exposure was down to $145 million for each percent move in rates. When the total portfolio had been liquidated, exposure was $22 million, negligible for a fund this size.

With all securities converted to cash, the initial $7.4 billion had shrunk to about $5.7 billion. Sleuthing auditors found additional assets worth $402 million, which were controlled by the pool but not listed on its formal investment inventories. Lenders repaid $40 million, and the liquidation returned $36 million more than expected. On the other side, $150 million of additional investor money was reported. Thus the estimated loss of $2,020 million was reduced to $1,690 million, but with an investor base now of $7,578 million. The losses are tallied in Table 9.3.

As these things go, the Orange County portfolio liquidation was a success. The sale earned $36 million more than expected. Substantial credit must go to Salomon Brothers, which efficiently auctioned off blocks of securities on a daily basis. Many structured notes were also sold back directly to the agencies that issued them, at an estimated benefit to the county of $10 million.

The portfolio benefited from improving conditions in the bond market. From December 13 to January 20, yields on short-term notes fell from 7.80% to 7.63%. Assuming an average duration of three years, the initial $9 billion portfolio gained about $45 million from this drop in rates. Part of the fall was due to the Mexican crisis, which led to a flight to "quality" issues (typically, U.S. government and agency bonds). The Fed was also magnanimous (no doubt unintentionally) and did not raise rates at its December 20 meeting.

All in all, OCIP had lost $1.69 billion dollars in the course of a year. Tom Hayes earned $67.24 an hour for his good work, plus travel expenses and a $152 per diem. Some of the lawyers, accountants, and other experts involved earned fees of up to $435 an hour. Hayes's assignment in Orange County ended on February 3, after which he left quickly: he had been hired by another municipal government (San Diego County's), which was suddenly worried about *its* investment pool.

10

Citron's Strategy (the Repo Man)

· · · · · · · · · · · · · · · · · · · ·

Before 1994, Robert Citron was one of the largest and most successful municipal investors in the United States. His bets on interest rates paid off handsomely, and his record won him a dangerous degree of freedom. Figure 10.1 compares the performance of OCIP with that of the state investment pool. During his 22 years of tenure, Citron delivered an average return of 9.4% whereas the state pool returned only 8.4%. In dollar terms, Bob Citron chalked up profits of *$755 million in excess of the state pool* (see Figure 10.2). His performance appeared truly exceptional.

Someone less successful than Citron would probably have been subjected to more independent oversight. His outsized returns on investment, delivered year after year, also made him feel comfortable with a degree of leverage that "lesser" fund managers would have found frightening.

Public agencies clamored to be admitted to OCIP. Only two cities in the county, Garden Grove and San Juan Capistrano, were not members, and they admitted to finding

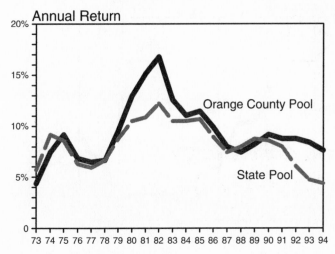

Figure 10.1 Performance of OCIP

Citron's returns "tempting." Even entities outside the county, such as the city of Beverly Hills, badly wanted in.

During the election campaign, in spring 1994, the Orange County chapter of the American Society of Public

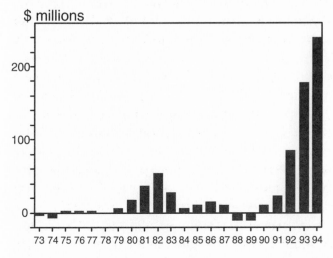

Figure 10.2 Additional Income of OCIP Compared to State Pool

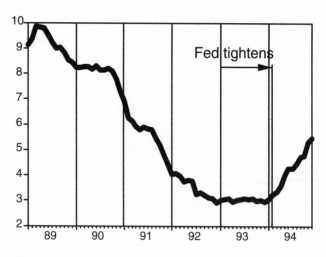

Figure 10.3 Path of Interest Rates

Accountants—not a bunch of fiscal lunatics, to be sure—gave Citron an award as an "outstanding public official." They praised his "exemplary contributions to government and the quality of life in Orange County." Only John Moorlach, whose criticisms were dismissed as mere partisan exaggeration, was less than convinced. "I think [Citron] is taking high risks," Moorlach said, sounding a little petulant. "I think he's cavalier. I think his portfolio, a lot of it, has been sheer luck."

That portfolio, on which the fiscal health of so many cities and public agencies depended, was supercharged with repurchase agreements and structured notes. These holdings essentially implemented a bet on *falling, or at least stable, interest rates*. As Figure 10.3 shows, this worked well from 1990 to 1993. But February 1994 was a turning point.

On February 4, 1994, the Federal Reserve Bank decided to increase a key interest rate from 3% to 3.25%. This "tightening" of monetary policy roiled the financial markets. Determined to slay another monster—inflation—the Fed raised interest rates no less than six times in 1994, which created a bloodbath in the bond market. And the OCIP portfolio started to take a battering. As Moorlach had predicted, the portfolio was "a major bull market bet in the middle of a bear market."

Still, Citron persisted in his risky strategy because of his belief that the U.S. economic recovery was fragile. (This misperception may have been because California remained in the economic doldrums while the rest of the country was expanding strongly.) Another reason for Citron's behavior may have been that the portfolio he had assembled was too complicated to be unwound fast enough to avoid incurring additional losses.

In any event, Citron believed in *holding to maturity*. Never mind that the market value of OCIP's assets was dropping due to rising rates; as long as enough cash was available to meet margin calls, OCIP's strategy would seem to work. Oh, and another minor detail, it would continue to work only as long as investors and lenders to the county did not ask for their money back.

Over the summer of 1994, the county and other local governments raised an additional $1.2 billion in short-term notes. These funds were immediately reinvested in bonds with maturities of up to 20 years and in inverse floaters. Citron put his strategy in play in a remarkably consistent fashion. First, he *leveraged the portfolio with $12.6 billion worth of repos, reinvesting the cash in notes or bonds*; second, he *increased the leverage even further by buying about $8 billion in structured notes*. He did hold to maturity most of the OCIP's bonds.

OCIP's leverage had increased steadily over time. Table 10.1, which shows this increase, does not, however, include other "side" accounts that were leveraged up to 13 times.

Citron also extended the duration of his investments in 1994, in effect trying to make up for previous losses. On October 4, for instance, he purchased $600 million worth of a

Table 10.1			
Leverage of OCIP			
Date	Holdings	Borrowings	Leverage
June 1990	3.5	1.7	1.5
June 1991	3.9	1.9	1.5
June 1992	5.6	3.9	1.7
June 1993	7.7	7.5	2.0
June 1994	9.4	12.7	2.3
November 1994	7.6	13.0	2.7

Sallie Mae note with a maturity of 10 years. This note had twice the maturity of most purchases, which was typically five years. Had some of this investment stayed in cash, Orange County might have avoided bankruptcy.

This "doubling up" strategy works more or less in this fashion. Imagine you are playing roulette in Las Vegas and you hit on the following scheme. In the first round, bet the minimum on black, say $10. If you win you get $20; your profit is $10, and you stop. If you lose, continue betting. In the second round, bet twice the first bet, $20 on black. If you win your return is $20; subtracting the $10 you lost before, your total profit is $20 − $10 = $10. You are ahead now and you stop. But if you lose, continue betting.

On the third round, bet four times the original amount, $40, on black. If you win your profit is $40 − $20 − $10 = $10, and you are ahead; if you lose, continue doubling the bet till you win.

Apparently, this "doubling up" strategy is a sure way to make money. The problem is that there may be a limit to your cash reserves. The amount you need to invest goes up very fast, indeed, at a geometric rate: starting with $10, after 10 rounds you will have to bet $5,120. Unless you have an unlimited line of credit, there is no guarantee you will be able to keep playing and recoup your losses.

This "doubling up" strategy, or something very much like it, failed for OCIP when cash reserves were almost exhausted and investors started pulling out their money. But there are other problems with the strategy, too. First, the "house" will always take a percentage of your winnings; for instance, you may win only $19 for every $10 you wager. (This is equivalent to a broker taking a fee for making a trade.) Transaction costs can transform a brilliant scheme into a losing proposition.

Second, the strategy assumes that the draws are "independent" over time; that is, each one has no effect on the one that follows. Although this is ideally the case in a game of roulette, interest rates movements often go in the same direction, as they did during 1994. As Merrill warned Citron, "Historically, the first Fed tightening has led to numerous others."

Indeed, one lesson we can perhaps draw from our example is that Robert Citron's great performance in the years before 1994 was due mostly to luck, not to investment skills. Forecasting interest rates is a notoriously difficult job. To bet on yields falling every year from 1990 to 1994 looks more like an *abdication* of the need to predict than anything else.

Before we enjoy ourselves too much, condemning Robert Citron for his financial errors, however, we should note that many other people, some in positions of great authority, agreed with Citron about OCIP's prospects.

John Moorlach's campaign, although unsuccessful, did succeed in stimulating a closer examination of the fund. There were at least four independent audits in 1994. None of these led to any sort of action to restrict the management of OCIP.

First, the Securities and Exchange Commission met with Citron and Raabe in April. The SEC has wide authority to oversee the nation's securities markets, and it also regulates the activities of brokers and dealers. Investigators found no evidence of illegal behavior; thus, no further action was taken, and the county Supervisors were not even notified of the investigation.

Second, Standard & Poor's and Moody's both re-examined the pool. After a detailed analysis of the pool, they reaffirmed their credit ratings for the county: just one notch below the highest possible. As of late spring, the county was still pondering whether to sue the rating agencies.

Third, the county's independent auditors, KPMG Peat Marwick, raised no flag during their annual audit (which was never finalized on account of the bankruptcy). County officials say the firm was supposed to assess potential weaknesses in internal controls as well as the portfolio itself. But Peat Marwick says that it was asked only to audit the portfolio, not to "second-guess the county's investment strategy."

Fourth, the county auditor, Steven Lewis, did not sound an alarm. More than a year before, Lewis had submitted a report to the county supervisors, covering the Treasurer's operations in 1991, in which he claimed that Citron had made some "risky and unusual transactions." He warned that Citron had invested in below-investment grade securities, which was in violation of the law; Citron later sold the offending securities. But Lewis did not address the issue of market risk, the root cause of OCIP's eventual downfall.

After December 1994, fund contributors and county bond buyers alike claimed to have been misled by Citron and Raabe. Indeed, the duo was less than forthcoming. In April, when asked what their strategy would be if rates were to continue rising, the answer was:

· ·

All investment managers have plans for changes in interest rates. However, you can't make plans for a worst-case scenario, because if you did, you would have to sacrifice any opportunity to earn a good return. . . . As money managers, it's our job to assess the most likely interest-rate risks and make plans accordingly. I can't discuss the specifics of my contingency plans, because part of an investment manager's strength in the investment markets is that the other investors don't know your plans. If they did, they could take investment positions that would allow them to take advantage of your needs.

· ·

As Citron testified at the January state Senate hearings, the plan was to hold to maturity. In addition, they repeatedly assured investors that they had enough liquidity to meet collateral call payments. Citron later pleaded guilty to six felony counts, including making misleading statements for the purpose of selling securities, misappropriating funds for the county, and falsifying accounting records. He was not accused of losing $1.7 billion.

However, much of the relevant information had been publicly available for a long time. Table 10.2 summarizes a portfolio report listing OCIP's holdings as of April 30, 1994. Such a report was made available to investors on a monthly basis; during the election, the reports were also sent to the press.

In the agency "fixed-rate note" category, the largest single holding was an $800 million position in a Fannie Mae note with a 5.41% coupon. From February to April 1994, the Fed had increased interest rates three times. Given a four year duration, this note alone had lost approximately 6% of

Table 10.2

Summarized OCIP Portfolio Statement for April 30, 1994

Asset	Face Value ($ million)	Cost ($ million)	Average Maturity
Treasury notes	582	591	4.5
Agency fixed-rate notes	8,480	8,493	4
Agency floating-rate notes	5,693	5,692	4
Corporate notes	1,912	1,912	4
Mortgage-backed securities	127	127	10
Certificates of deposit	1,609	1,609	4
Mutual funds	421	421	NA
Discount notes	686	683	0
Commercial paper	350	349	0
Total securities	19,860	19,879	
Reverse RP	−12,529	−11,833	
Net	7,331	8,046	
Leverage	2.71		

its value. Using the figure of 2.71 for leverage, this suggests a loss of 16%—not far from the eventual loss of 22% on the pool.

The report clearly lists all securities, broken down by category, and indicates the face value, cost, purchase date, maturity, and so forth. The only items not immediately easy to evaluate from the report are those in the "agency floating-rate note" category, which contained such securities as floating rate notes, inverse floaters, and other structured notes. A typical listing is

Item	Purchase Date	Maturity Date	CUSIP
$800 million FNMA 5.41% 6/98	07-01-93	6-25-98	31364AZL9

Hence, all securities were listed in a typical OCIP report, including even the "CUSIP" number that provides a unique identification for each. Therefore, the argument from insufficient information is hard to sustain. No doubt the riskiness of Citron's management is much easier to recognize now, with 20-20 hindsight. But some individuals, such as candidate John Moorlach, were able to look at reports like the one displayed previously and formulate highly accurate predictions of default and disaster. Many people *wanted* such predictions not to be true, despite their own exposure to risk; and the great principle, widely popularized under President Ronald Reagan, of "If it ain't broke, don't fix it," was once again improperly applied.

Moorlach's campaign was curiously ineffective because of his failure or inability to provide documentation supporting his charges against Citron. None of his financial advisors was willing to be identified, which must have affected the credibility of the campaign. According to one report, they did not want to antagonize Mr. Citron, who was a major player in financial markets. Others have said that they were afraid of taking on Merrill, which was closely associated with Citron. Perhaps this lack of supporting information was why Moorlach's campaign was viewed as "politically motivated."

Naive investors, such as local school boards, are hard to fault for a lack of financial savvy. But the people who advised such organizations laid claim to sufficient expertise, and they were confident in their endorsements of Citron. As we know, some school districts and local cities not only invested their revenues in OCIP, they *borrowed* money so as to invest more than they had (i.e., leveraged their own positions). The city of Irvine, for example, issued a general obligation taxable note, worth $62 million, in July 1994 and invested the proceeds immediately in OCIP, at an estimated profit of $1.2 million. Jeff Niven, the city's investment chief, said later that the agencies who rated Irvine's bonds (S&P's, Moody's) had given them their highest grade, *but only on condition that Niven deposit the proceeds in OCIP.* Thus the impulse to invest was not only endorsed, but in some cases required, by institutions known to be expert at evaluating risk.

More savvy investors should have known better. Peer Swan, the chairman of the Irvine Water Ranch District (IRWD), was a strong supporter of Citron during the election campaign, accusing Moorlach of "yelling 'Fire' in a crowded theater." During the campaign, he complained that Moorlach criticisms had increased the cost of borrowing by $12,000 for a $30 million debt issue for the IRWD. Swan declared that finance officers in his agency looked closely at the OCIP before investing $400 million, even "simulating an increase in interest rates to see if their money would be safe." Interestingly, Swan was one of the first investors to pull out money from the pool in November.

Overall, many municipal officials failed to follow basic rules of investing. They *failed to understand OCIP's strategy; neglected to look closely at the instruments being employed;* and *declined to question OCIP's extraordinary results.* These are basic mistakes; they come from addiction to success, and they probably have little to do with the "baffling" complexity of derivatives. Consider that the Board of Supervisors, whose responsibility it was to oversee the County Treasurer, probably never read the report Steve Lewis, the county auditor, sent them in August 1993. When told of the existence of this (mildly) critical report, Supervisor Roger Stanton said, "My God! Was it addressed to the board?" And Supervisor Harriet Wieder added, "What? You're kidding. I'm sitting here with my mouth open. I'm absolutely shocked."

Table 10.3

Breaking down OCIP's Losses

Instrument	Value (billion)	Return (Jan–Nov 94)	Loss (million)
Initial portfolio	$7.6		
Fixed-rate notes	$12.0	−3.0%	$360
Inverse floaters	$8.0	−7.8%	$620
Borrowing costs	$12.4	−5.0%	$620
Total portfolio:			
Loss estimate		−21%	$1,600
Salomon's actual loss		−22%	$1,690

With all the pieces of the financial puzzle in place, we can now tally the losses in Table 10.3.

The $12 billion invested in fixed-rate notes had an average maturity of four years. From December 1993 to November 1994, interest rates increased from 5.2% to 7.8%. Taking into account price movement and accrued interest, a four-year note lost about 3% in value over this period—hence a loss of $360 million.

Assume next that $8 billion was invested in a five-year inverse floater. As explained in the "structured notes" chapter, its value drops by 12.8% for a 2.5% rise in yield. With a 5% coupon payment, the total loss on the inverse floater is 7.8%, which translates into a dollar loss of $620 million.

Finally, we must account for short-term borrowing costs. Assuming an amount of $12.4 billion, and imputing a short-term average borrowing cost of 5%, we arrive at additional costs of $620 million. This yields a total loss estimate of $1,600 million, fairly close to the Salomon estimate of $1,690 million.

To sum up, Robert Citron took extraordinary risks with the taxpayers' money. This is hard to explain in the usual way. Typically, such gambles are taken by traders who reap a personal bonus based on profits or hedge fund managers who receive performance fees in the neighborhood of 20% of profits. But this may be the only example in contemporary financial history of a government official taking extreme risks from which he stood not to benefit at all in the monetary sense. In fact, as has been noted, Citron derived personal political benefits from his actions.

Instead of speculating about Citron's personal motives, it may be sufficient to note that a big ego is the one quality *not* recommended for people dealing in financial markets. Traders burdened with too much ego, upon taking a loss, tend to blame the market for the wrong turning, and sometimes they *increase* an unpromising position. This is why bank traders are carefully supervised, their positions subject to strict limits and evaluated at least once a day. Good traders can almost be said to have *no* ego. They recognize their mistakes and cut their losses when necessary.

Suing Wall Street

. . . .

On January 12, 1995, Orange County filed a $2.4 billion lawsuit against Merrill Lynch, charging the brokerage house with "wantonly and callously" selling the county highly risky securities in violation of state and federal laws. This lawsuit is but the largest in a series of suits related to the bankruptcy. The holders of Orange County bonds have also sued Merrill and Citron. And the county has sued one of the brokers that hastily liquidated its collateral.

The bankruptcy filing under Chapter 9 temporarily prevents investors from suing the county. Still, it is clear that the net beneficiaries in this affair will be the lawyers. As soon as news of the bankruptcy broke, pin-striped attorneys began arriving at Orange County's John Wayne airport. In a so-called beauty contest held December 16, attorneys competed for clients among the county's creditors, and more than a third of the 50 largest firms in the state found employment. As one counselor put it, "There are kids running around in Orange County in junior high today who will be joining this case once they get through law school."

The county claims Merrill bears a heavy responsibility for the $1.7 billion loss. The rapid growth of Merrill's municipal finance business has been achieved by aggressive sales. Merrill dominates the market now and was the top municipal underwriter in 1994 (with 11.6% of the market). The success of the firm stems from both size and diversification. Merrill can easily sell the bonds it underwrites as part of its own mutual funds and through its network of retail brokers. Merrill is also very profitable. In 1994, it earned $1 billion on revenues of $9.6 billion. Because it is so large, Merrill is also a great target for lawsuits.

Robert Citron had a close working relationship with Michael Stamenson, one of Merrill's top sales representatives. With his junior partners, Debra Harris and Duane Canaga, Stamenson sold products to many California treasurers from his office in San Francisco. Stamenson and Citron shared a comfort with risk that perhaps was ill-suited to the needs of conservative public agencies. The finance director for the city of San Mateo, for example, declined to do business with Stamenson because of his trading style. Brokers, of course, have an incentive to trade actively—this is how they generate business. Full-service brokers like Stamenson routinely provide market opinions while also pushing their products. To ask them to behave otherwise is to ask them not to be what they are.

Still, Stamenson has had his share of controversy. He was the lead figure in a previous municipal investment debacle, in which the city of San Jose lost $60 million in a bold leverage scheme. When asked whether the securities he sold were too risky for public agencies, Stamenson replied curtly: "Risk means different things at different times to different people."

The lawsuit against Merrill centers on two issues. The first is the question of *adequate warning*. Specifically, did Merrill alert OCIP to the risk of its position vis-à-vis interest rates? Merrill says that it did: beginning in October 1992, Merrill warned Citron, in writing, of the unhappy consequences should rates go up. Merrill even proposed to buy back, at a profit to the county, $3.5 billion in structured notes it had sold OCIP. When Citron declined to accept this offer, Stamenson wrote that he "would not and could not represent that Orange County should base its portfolio strategy exclusively on Merrill interest rate projections." This seems a pretty clear-cut warning (and also possibly an attempt by Stamenson to cover himself, should there be lawsuits in the future).

Merrill also claims that in February 1994 it provided an analysis showing that the county's structured notes would drop in value by $270 million for every one-point rise in rates. Merrill also recommended that OCIP either sell its riskiest securities or buy structured notes designed to profit from rising rates.

The county views things differently. Only a week after this report, Citron had a breakfast meeting with Stamenson and Charles Clough, at which Clough told Citron that high interest rates were "not sustainable." The county also claims that subsequent sales by Merrill were inconsistent with this position (that is, warnings to divest). Between October 1992 and November 1994, Merrill sold the county an additional $2.8 billion worth of products whose value was negatively related to interest rates. A reasonable defense would be to say that a broker simply arranges transactions for independent investors, who then have a right to choose a particular interest-rate scenario. Merrill took the view that Citron's strategy had been made public and endorsed in the election campaign. A Merrill spokesperson declared that, "This reminds me a little of that old line in Casablanca: 'There was gambling going on here? I'm shocked!'"

The other issue central to the suit against Merrill is *suitability*. Although not precisely defined, the concept of suitability figures in securities laws designed to protect clients, such as the proverbial widows and orphans, from brokers pushing speculative instruments.

The county argued that some of Merrill's sales were so unsuitable as to be illegal. The so-called *ultra vires* claim has been used successfully against brokers in other cases: it says that decades of legal precedent preclude a municipality from incurring any debt that exceeds that year's revenues, absent special approval of the electorate. The city of San Jose brought an *ultra vires* action against Merrill (and others) at the time of the $60 million leverage scheme mentioned previously. Merrill and other firms settled out of court.

More recently, a West Virginia municipal pool lost $279 million from investments in Treasury securities (see Box 11.1). A circuit court judge ruled that the investments were illegal on *ultra vires* grounds, but Wall Street is appealing the verdict.

Box 11.1 West Virginia's Story

History has a way of repeating itself. Witness the story of West Virginia's Consolidated Investment Fund, which announced a loss of about $300 million in 1987.

Until 1987, the $1.2 billion fund was one of the best performing in the nation. It attracted many local agencies to the pool. By trading in long-maturity securities, the pool was betting on falling interest rates. This strategy worked perfectly in 1985 and 1986. In 1987, though, rates started to rise and created "paper" losses in the portfolio. In an attempt to make up these losses, managers increased their exposure through reverse repos. So far, the similarities between the West Virginia and Orange County cases are striking.

As rates increased further, from 7.1% in January to a high of 9.5% in October, portfolio managers sold securities to make their collateral call payments. News of the loss led to a run on the fund and the resignation of the state treasurer. The state also sued securities dealers. A number of brokers, including Merrill, Salomon, and Goldman Sachs, settled out of court for $28 million, but Morgan Stanley contested the suit.

On a motion for summary judgment, a state trial court held that Morgan Stanley had knowingly helped the portfolio managers to engage in transactions that were prohibited by West Virginia law, for which it awarded the state a total of about $52 million.

The crux of the problem was that the trades apparently violated specific state rules against speculation, against investing in long-maturity bonds, and against selling options. Morgan Stanley had tried to persuade the treasurer to repeal the prohibition on speculation but was unsuccessful. The broker allegedly continued to trade with the fund, buying and selling as much as $20 billion in five months. This was eminently profitable: assuming transaction costs of 0.25%, all this trading translates into revenues of $50 million.

On appeal, however, West Virginia's highest court reversed the award, holding that Morgan Stanley was entitled to a jury trial on the issue of whether it had helped the state engage in "speculation." The court also held that, in a fiduciary context, losses that occur through innocent violations of laws "may, nonetheless, be offset by gains achieved at roughly the same time by the same type of violations." In other words, the court clearly thought that it is not fair for the state to keep the profits from illegal trades but transfer the losses from the same kinds of trades to Morgan Stanley. In addition, the court said, in effect, that it was unfair to try to drag deep-pocket defendants from another state to court in West Virginia, where any jury was bound to favor the home team.

Clearly, Merrill had a highly profitable relationship with Orange County. According to the suit filed by the county, Merrill earned nearly $100 million in underwriting fees, trading commissions, and other charges from its dealings with the county in 1993 and 1994 alone. Over these two years, Merrill's profit margin from dealings with the county (net

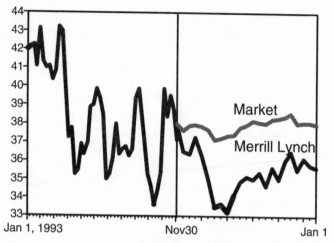

Figure 11.1 The Impact of the Orange County Crisis on Merrill

income over net revenues) amounted to 20%. Bob Citron's business was a lucrative one.

For an idea of how these profits came about, consider this. In November, one month before the bankruptcy, Merrill underwrote a $600 million note from Sallie Mae. Orange County absorbed the whole issue for a price of $100.628 per $100 in face value. The day of the sale, Bloomberg Financial Services assessed the value of these notes at $96.897, suggesting that Citron had paid too much. Merrill's revenues from this trade alone have been estimated at $2 to $6 million.

In the two days following the bankruptcy, Merrill's stock plunged from $37.75 to $34.50. Figure 11.1 graphs the movements in Merrill's stock price and compares it to movements in the stock market, as measured by the S&P 500 index. We can conclude from Figure 11.1 that most of the fall in Merrill stock value was due to perceptions of its role vis-à-vis Orange County, since the rest of the market did not plunge in the same way. After stabilizing, Merrill's stock price had fallen overall by about $2.00. With 193 million common shares outstanding, Merrill's stock drop thus translated into a loss of about $400 million in market value. This is the market's estimate of the impact of the bankruptcy on Merrill. One might even say that this is the market's estimate of the future cost to Merrill of the bankruptcy, in terms both of business lost and legal fees to come.

Merrill's attitude to its relationship with Bob Citron is intriguing, to say the least. The risk management unit at Merrill, headed by Daniel Napoli, has been long concerned about the large exposure of Merrill to the OCIP. The repurchase desk, headed by Gary Rupert, was also worried about the risk of default. Napoli even paid a personal visit to Citron in February 1992 to discuss his concern about the leverage of the fund. This led to Stamenson's first official letter of warning to Citron in October 1992. Over the following months, however, Citron leveraged the portfolio even further. The medium-term desk, which sold billions of agency notes, was only too happy to oblige. Apparently, there were differences of opinion within Merrill between the risk management and the sales groups, and even within these groups, about what and how much to sell to Citron. Some Merrill executives justified subsequent sales on the grounds that the notes were less leveraged than before. Since these sales could not have been made without the approval of Merrill's top management, it is also conceivable that the firm's top executives believed Citron had been provided sufficient warnings.

Orange County filed for bankruptcy in a desperate attempt to avoid sale of the securities held as collateral. Yet the Wall Street investment houses went ahead and liquidated the entire $11 billion position anyhow.

Orange County then filed suit against Nomura Securities, which had liquidated about $900 million worth of securities. Bankruptcy filing under Chapter 9 provides a statutory injunction, called an *automatic stay*, that—at least in theory—prevents creditors from selling the assets of a bankrupt entity.

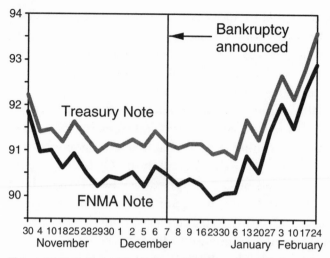

Figure 11.2 Comparative Prices of FNMA and Treasury Notes

But the bankruptcy code is vague on the question of whether repos are subject to automatic stay; indeed, Congress explicitly exempted repos from automatic stay under Chapter 11. Whether repos are exempt under Chapter 9 is a thorny legal issue that will likely be resolved in the courts.

One week after the bankruptcy announcement, the county itself decided to liquidate the remaining $9 billion portfolio, thus rendering the issue moot. The motion was approved by the bankruptcy court. To analyze the effect of this decision, consider the price of two nearly identical notes, one issued by an agency and the other by the Treasury. Figure 11.2 plots the price of the FNMA issue of November 1998, with a 5.05% coupon, and the Treasury note of November 1998, with a 5.125% coupon. The FNMA note was bought at par, that is, $100, and was valued at $90.67 on December 6, when the Wall Street brokers liquidated. During the county's liquidation (after December 13), the note's value fell to about $90. Therefore, the county realized a loss of roughly 10% by selling when it did.

As it happened, December was the worst possible time to sell. The bond market recovered in the following months; the FNMA note went back up to $96.81 by the end of June. Its yield fell from 8% to 6.1%. Using the state auditor's duration of 7.4 years, the portfolio would have gained 7.4 years times $7.5 billion times (8% − 6.1%), which is about $1,050 million. *Had the liquidation of the pool been avoided, the portfolio would have recovered about $1,050 million out of the $1,700 million loss.* Bob Citron, if he noticed, was probably bitterly disappointed. (This, however, is hindsight again; and the outcome could have been very different. Had interest rates continued to rise, selling in December would have looked very good.)

The important lesson is that, in cases such as this, involving leverage, liquidation may be forced when the market drops, margin calls accumulate, and cash reserves are drying up. If there is any mean-reversion in interest rates (the tendency for rates not to go too high or too low, returning to a "mean" value in the absence of high inflation), then margin calls will force selling at the worst possible point.

As for the sale by the New York brokers, was this made at distressed prices, too? To answer such a question, we need to look more closely at the relationship between agency and Treasury notes. Agencies have slightly higher yields than equivalent Treasury issues in part because of perception of credit risk. The difference in yields is called the *yield spread* (see Figure 11.3). The yield spread between these issues had been around 0.31% but spiked up to 0.38% on December 6, when the brokers started to sell, and then again later in the month, when Tom Hayes sold chunks of the portfolio.

The difference in yields (0.38% − 0.31%, or 7 basis points) represents a *temporary drop* in the value of the agency notes due to selling. How much does this represent in dollars? If you recall our discussion of duration (in Chapter 3), the price drop will be equal to the portfolio value times its duration times the increase in yield. If we assume that the

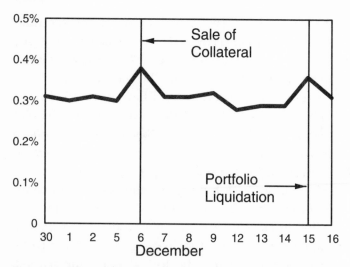

Figure 11.3 Impact of the Sale: FNMA–Treasury Yield Spread

whole portfolio behaved like this particular issue, then the price drop was $56 million (for a $20 billion portfolio with a duration of four years). The loss was probably even greater, due to the sale of structured notes, which are costly to trade and generally sell at lower prices than fixed-rate notes. Remember, this was an *additional* loss, having nothing to do with the general increase in interest rates and the resulting decline in the market value of notes. It was caused by the liquidation of collateral itself.

All in all, the liquidation of the portfolio led to a temporary price drop of $56 million, transaction costs of at least $50 million, and legal fees of $24 million until June. Bankruptcy will cost the county easily more than $100 million. Whether any of this will be recovered from Wall Street remains to be seen.

12

The Bondholders
. . . .

"There are no guarantees in really any financial market. All you can look behind is the underlying credit"

JEFF NIVEN, MANAGER OF FINANCIAL SERVICES, CITY OF IRVINE
. . . .

O range County was nobody's idea of a bad bet. As one of the most prosperous areas in the nation, it issued bonds that investors felt safe buying. The bond-rating agencies agreed: as late as September 19, Standard & Poor's was assigning its highest short-term rating (A1+) to the county's $110 million of notes. When the bankruptcy came, therefore, a severe shock went through the municipal market—more severe than if some second-rate issuing body had gone under. Munis immediately dropped in price relative to Treasuries, reflecting widespread doubt about the market in general. In effect, this raised the cost of capital for all municipalities around the country. This is quite a large market. In 1993, $280 billion was raised by municipalities.

S&P's and Moody's long-term credit ratings for the county were also close to the highest possible: AA and Aa1, respectively. The agencies claimed to have conducted a thorough examination of OCIP, yet they remained unaware of the impending cash crisis. This highlights an important problem with the ratings agencies. In general, *the agencies focus only on credit risk*; that is, the possibility that a borrower will fail to repay. But this is the view that led the OCIP, like many other investors, to buy agency debt, supposedly safe from default but certainly not from market risk. The ratings agencies failed to recognize that market risk can *lead* to credit risk.

As an example of a similar telescoping of market and credit risk, consider the overseas debt crisis of the 1980s. American (and other) commercial banks had been eager to lend to developing countries like Brazil and Mexico, but they hoped to escape exposure to currency, interest, and credit risk. An instrument known as the *syndicated Eurodollar loan* seemed to provide an answer. It was denominated in dollars (no currency risk), was payable on a floating rate basis (no interest risk), and was made to governments (which were unlikely to go out of business). But after U.S. interest rates skyrocketed in the early 1980s, countries like Mexico and Brazil went into default: they were unable to make the (floating) interest payments on their loans. In short, market risk had turned into credit risk, and on a huge scale.

Following the bankruptcy announcement in December, Moody's downgraded Orange County's long-term debt to level Caa (below investment grade). And S&P changed its AA rating to CCC, which one wag said stood for "colossal California catastrophe."

Types of Bonds

The bankruptcy had different impacts on different kinds of bonds and issuers. Bond issued by the county, local municipalities, and agencies include the following:

1. *General obligation bonds.* These are unsecured, backed only by the full faith and taxing authority of the borrower.
2. *Revenue bonds.* These are payable from the revenue generated by special facilities (e.g., toll bridges or sewage installations).
3. *Redevelopment bonds.* These are financed by new tax revenues from redevelopment areas.
4. *Mello-Roos bonds* (also called *dirt bonds*). These are issued for infrastructure projects such as school construction, financed by real estate taxes in a particular area.
5. *Certificates of participation.* Here bondholders participate in lease payments made to the bond issuer.

Generally, revenue bonds are considered risky, because a particular revenue stream may dry up. General obligation bonds, backed by the full taxing authority of the municipality, are usually viewed as safer and therefore pay lower yields. But, in the Orange County case, this situation was reversed: the *revenue bonds* had first access to a pool of dedicated funds coming from specific investments. This was a requirement of bankruptcy filing under Chapter 9. Holders of nonrevenue bonds were named as *unsecured* creditors, meaning payment would come only after county employees, some suppliers, bankruptcy attorneys, and federal debt had already been paid.

The main distinguishing feature of municipal bonds is their *tax exemption.* This exemption derives from the constitutional doctrine of reciprocal immunity: state and local governments do not tax federal property, and the federal government reciprocates in kind. As a result, investors require lower interest on municipal debt. This allows municipalities to raise funds at relatively low cost.

Table 12.1

Bonds Issued by Orange County

Type of Bond	Amount ($ million)
Short-term taxable notes	600
Tax revenue anticipation notes	200
Property tax notes	175
Pension obligation bond	320
Certificate of participation	474
Total	1,769

Source: *Wall Street Journal*, February 9, 1995.

However, municipalities can now issue *taxable* as well as tax-free debt. This is an effect of the Tax Reform Act of 1986, which sought to curb abuses of the tax-exempt status. Tax-exempt status is now restricted to issues for strictly "public purposes," such as road building or school construction.

In the summer of 1994, when the Orange County Investment Pool was running low on cash, Robert Citron arranged for a $600 million *taxable* note issue (underwritten by Merrill Lynch). His main purpose was to generate cash for the pool, perhaps to meet collateral margin calls that were starting to mount dangerously. (In April 1995, Citron pled guilty to several felony charges, some of which related to an incomplete disclosure of risks to investors in that $600 million issue.) This issuance was relatively unusual, because taxable debt is expensive for a municipality, and was motivated by a looming cash crunch. Table 12.1 breaks down the bonds issued by the county.

As of May, the county was still paying interest on its outstanding bonds, but it was technically in default on $110 million in taxable floating rate notes issued in September

Table 12.2

Mutual Funds' Holdings in Orange County

Fund	Amount in OC Debt ($ million)	Total Amount ($ million)	Percent Exposed
Franklin CA Tax-Free Income	229	13,478	1.7
Putnam CA Tax-Exempt Income	72	2,266	3.2
CMA Tax Exempt	69	5,219	1.3
Alliance Municipal Income CA	66	1,024	6.4
Allstate Insurance Co.	45	14,986	0.3
Franklin CA Ins. Tax-Free Income	44	1,428	3.1
Smith Barney CA Muni	32	642	5.0
Merrill Lynch CA Muni Bond	24	800	3.0
Dean Witter CA Tax Free	23	1,100	2.1
Putnam Tax-Free High Yield	23	1,560	1.5
California IT Tax-Free Income	21	236	8.9

Source: CDA Investment Technologies.

(originally held by CS First Boston). These notes contained the put option that, when exercised in December, precipitated the crisis. Furthermore, the county was facing the repayment of the $600 million taxable note, for which it had insufficient funds.

Mutual funds were also invested in debt issued by Orange County agencies. Those holding at least $20 million worth are listed in Table 12.2. Fortunately, a large proportion of these bonds were protected by private insurance. Insurers such as the Municipal Bond Investors Assurance Corp. guarantee that, in the event of a default, both the interest and principal will be paid on time. The Monday after the bankruptcy, the Association of Financial Guaranty Insurors took out a full-page ad in the *Wall Street Journal*, trumpeting the value of insurance for municipal bonds (about 40% of new issues are now insured).

The bankrupcty highlighted two aspects of municipal bond funds. The first is the power of diversification. Investors who invested heavily in OC's debt were badly burned. Mutual funds allow investors to spread their risk across many borrowers.

The second aspect relates to the choice of funds organized on a statewide or multistate basis. Statewide funds provide tax advantages for investors in high tax brackets, because they allow deductibility of interest at the federal *and* state levels. For example, say that a California municipal bond offers a yield of 5%. This is taken after tax. For those in the highest income tax brackets, 39.6% for federal taxes and 11% for California, the effective rate of taxation is 39.6% plus $11\% \times (1 - 39.6\%)$ because state taxes can be deducted at the federal level. Therefore, the effective total tax (bracket) is 46.2%. To find the equivalent before-tax interest, we divide the tax-exempt yield by one minus the tax bracket:

Effective Taxable Interest	=	Tax-exempt Interest	÷	1 − Tax Bracket

In this example, a 5% tax-exempt yield translates into an effective tax yield of $5.00\% / (1 - 46.2\%) = 9.30\%$ for a California resident in the highest tax bracket. For a resident of another state, the effective yield is $5.00\% / (1 - 39.6\%) = 8.28\%$, considerably lower.

To decide whether to invest in taxable or nontaxable investments, compare this effective yield with what could be obtained from a taxable investment. If taxable funds have lower yields, then a municipal bond might be a good investment.

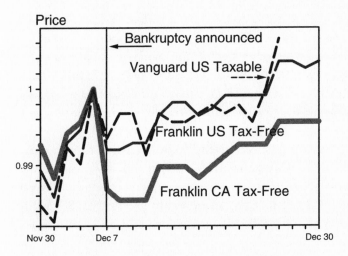

Price

Bankruptcy announced

Vanguard US Taxable

Franklin US Tax-Free

Franklin CA Tax-Free

1 -

0.99 -

Nov 30   Dec 7   Dec 30

Figure 12.1 Effect of the Bankruptcy on Municipal Funds

An important caveat applies here. The two investments, taxable and nontaxable, must be equivalent in terms
of market and credit risk. It does not make sense to compare
the yield on a 30-year municipal with that on a 1-year corporate bond. Also, an investor needs to make sure that no
hidden feature, such as a call option, might artificially increase the yield. Finally, the credit risk of the two bonds
must be the same.

Note that the higher effective taxable yield, 9.30% instead of 8.28%, for California residents is obtained at the
expense of less diversification across states. If the state economy turns sour, as it did in the early 1990s, there will be more
defaults in the state than in the rest of the nation. Therefore,
the additional effective yield must be carefully balanced
against higher credit risk due to concentrating in one state.
Multiple-state funds were less affected than California-only
funds in December 1994.

The price effects of the bankruptcy are suggested by
Figure 12.1, which plots the fortunes of three bond funds

with an average maturity around 20 years. The three funds are *Franklin California Tax-Free Fund*, with holdings in municipal bonds issued by the state of California or California agencies; *Franklin U.S. Tax-Free Fund*, with holdings in municipal bonds issued all over the country; and *Vanguard Long-Term Federal Fund*, with holdings in taxable Treasury issues. Figure 12.1 scales the value of the funds to $1.00 on the day before the bankruptcy. Relative to other funds, the Franklin California Fund lost about 1%. CS First Boston, in a more systematic study, found that between December 6 and February 1, national municipal funds appreciated by 3% while California municipal funds appreciated by 1.8%, a difference of 1.2%.

The state of California has refused to take fiscal responsibility for the Orange County debacle. This is understandable but perhaps unwise, because all California municipalities will be facing higher capital costs if the bond market decides the state will never back any of its local governments. Matt Fong, the California state treasurer, has warned that California municipalities may have to pay hundreds of millions more a year in financing costs if investors require a higher return on California paper.

Many individual investors suffered directly from the bankruptcy. Some of these are retired investors who depend on interest payments for subsistence. The market for Orange County bonds froze after December; no one wanted to buy them or, more precisely, the prices at which they could have sold were so low that no one wanted to deal. In February, after a two month hiatus, county debt started trading again at 82 cents on the dollar. This is a loss of 18% of principal.

In July 1994, the county and other agencies issued $1.2 billion in taxable notes; at that time, the pool had already suffered considerable losses. The proceeds from the issue were immediately reinvested in new securities. The value of these notes has now plunged. Irate investors claim that they were misled about the condition of the pool.

According to the bondholders' lawsuit, the prospectus for the Merrill-led issue mentioned that the cash would go into a leveraged pool; furthermore, that the fund's value did not necessarily represent its worth. But the fund's unrealized losses were never mentioned. Federal securities laws require municipalities to reveal "material information" that might affect the value of their debt. The issue of whether the buyers of these notes were the victims of fraud will be settled in court. This lawsuit is part of a wider search for culprits in the Orange County affair.

13

Placing Blame

· · · · · · · · · · · · · · · · ·

The Beleaguered Supervisors

Orange County does not have a chief executive. When the county incorporated in 1889, it chose a governmental structure consisting of five elected supervisors; the purpose of this incorporation—somewhat ironic, in light of developments a century later—was to secure tighter control of tax revenues raised locally.

As we saw in a previous chapter, the Supervisors are subject to antiquated "sunshine laws" that prohibit meetings without advance public notice. The inefficiency resulting from this was one of the factors behind the bankruptcy. During the negotiations to sell the funds' assets, for instance, the Supervisors had to be kept in separate rooms and informed individually of developments. In this era of instantly moving capital flows, a few hours of delays can be disastrous.

The two oldest Supervisors, Thomas Riley and Harriet Wieder, were due to retire in December, 1994, and their inattention to the impending crisis was perhaps attributable to a reluctance to rock the boat near the end of a long voyage. Riley, a former Marine general, and Wieder, a career politician, have publicly indicated that the Board did not supervise Citron closely in part because of his winning record. They have also claimed that they did not receive crucial information about the pool that would have apprised them of the risks Citron was taking. The supervisors who had no directly relevant experience, William Steiner, a former director of a home for abused children, and Gaddi Vasquez, a former policeman, noticed nothing amiss. Steiner has said that he did not recall seeing the 1993 audit, but that it "should have been a huge red flag." Vasquez has said that "there were no glaring signs or signals being transmitted that something was awry." Even Supervisor Roger Stanton, who as a full professor of management at California State University, Long Beach, had more than a passing aquaintance with issues of government finance, claimed that he was misled by reports indicating that the fund was sound.

Even so, the board's reaction to John Moorlach is instructive. On May 31, near the end of his campaign for treasurer, Moorlach sent an eight-page letter to the Supervisors, reiterating the warnings he had given throughout the campaign. Among other points, he argued that the OCIP portfolio was heavily invested in inverse floaters, which have a lower yield when interest rates rise; that the pool had already answered heavy collateral calls, adding to a loss of value of up to $1.2 billion; that Citron's plan in case of trouble was to increase leverage and hold to maturity, a recipe for disaster. Moorlach also wrote, "I would strongly recommend that you prepare for a worst case scenario." And he concluded, "Should you have any questions . . . please do not hesitate to contact me."

Moorlach says nobody ever called him back. No doubt Moorlach's tone of urgency was laid to partisanship; his letter, although carefully written, was also belligerent in tone (your "tacit approval" of Citron, he told Supervisor Riley, is like "sticking your head in the sand"). Supervisor Riley, a former Marine general, must not have been pleased to receive this letter. As we have seen, Orange County had benefited handsomely from Citron's investments during periods of low interest rates; the treasurer's long history of success may have inclined the Supervisors to doubt any criticisms or, perhaps we should say, to *hope strongly* that any criticisms were wrong. After all, Citron had made the Supervisors' political lives easy: they could win election as enemies of taxation while running a government awash in revenues.

This also explains the rubber-stamp approval of the $600 million taxable note issue in July 1994. At the state Senate hearings in January, Vasquez and Stanton were grilled about their monitoring of county finances. (Gaddi Vasquez, a former police officer, rose to national prominence as a speaker at the 1988 GOP convention and, at some point, was considered a rising star in the Republican party.) Vasquez, unaccustomed to such a hostile audience, said he could not recall details of the transaction. Then one of the inquisitors pulled up a tape recorder and played a one-minute segment showing that the item was passed on the Supervisors' *consent* calendar with no discussion. Later, Stanton explained that the board was led astray by the advice of county staff and financial experts, who indicated that the investment pool was in good health. Also, the Supervisors felt they had little authority or control over the treasurer, by virtue of the fact that Citron was directly elected by the public.

After the bankruptcy, the Supervisors became a focus of popular resentment. Community activists began a campaign demanding the resignation of the three board members present during the crisis (Roger Stanton, William Steiner, and Gaddi Vasquez) who remained in office. A period of posturing and blame deflection ensued, during which the Supervisors made clear their adamant opposition to higher taxes, thus regaining the support of some of their harshest critics. Later, confronted with a gaping budget deficit, the board agreed to put a sales tax on the ballot, but two Supervisors said they would not vote for it.

Arms of the Law

After news of the bankruptcy hit, a number of investigators went into action.

The Securities and Exchange Commission (SEC) subpoenaed Citron, Raabe, the five Supervisors, Ernie Schneider (the chief administrative officer of the county), and Merrill's brokers. The federal agency wanted to investigate securities laws violations and whether improper campaign contributions or kickbacks were given to county officials. In June 1994, for instance, three Merrill brokers each gave $1,000 to Citron's re-election campaign. (Merrill claims these donations were legal.) It seems unlikely, anyhow, that Citron engaged in a $20 billion interest rate bet because he received $3,000 in contributions.

Strictly speaking, regulation of local investment pools is not a federal matter. SEC commissioner Richard Roberts has recommended that the states tighten their own rules, and he has advised bondholders "to sue."

The Commodity Futures Trading Commission (CFTC) also began an investigation. The CFTC is a sister institution to the SEC and has jurisdiction over exchange-traded derivatives. The CFTC wanted to determine whether the OCIP held futures and, if so, whether federal regulations were followed.

Other investigations undertaken: the National Association of Securities Dealers (NASD), a trade organization, began an examination of the campaign contributions by Merrill brokers; the U.S. Attorney's office began checking into whether the U.S. mail or phone wires were used to defraud investors; and the Orange County District Attorney's office, under Michael Capizzi, began looking at how the pool was run and what representations were made to OCIP participants. Capizzi's agents seized 50 boxes of documents from the Treasurer's and Auditor's offices, and he also directed a raid on Citron's home. In May, Citron pleaded guilty to six felony counts and Raabe was indicted on similar grounds.

The Treasurer's Office

When Arthur Andersen & Co., an accounting firm, began combing through OCIP's disorganized records, they found an additional $402 million belonging to the fund. A less pleasant discovery, formally announced on January 21, was that $108 million in interest income had been diverted from pool participants and toward two county-owned accounts. The skimming of income was done by inflating the interest allocated to the county and by improper transfers, later blamed on a "computer programming error."

The auditors found no evidence of embezzlement or missing funds. One of the accounts, an Economic Uncertainty Fund, had been set up in 1993 to handle excess interest earned by the pool. Money in the fund had been used for public library needs, fire services, and other routine public expenditures. The purpose of the other fund, Number 99J, was less clear. It had been set up as a participant's account but without a designated participant.

Matthew Raabe, acting treasurer following Citron's resignation, declined to answer questions about the two accounts. As a result, the Supervisors placed him on administrative leave, along with two of his top aides. On February 25, both Raabe and Chief Administrative Officer Schneider were fired. Schneider later described himself as "a classic scapegoat" who had been victimized by the Supervisors.

On January 27, auditors also revealed that $271 million in losses suffered by a county fund had been improperly shifted to other participants in the pool. Initially, the county fund, Number 100, contained $250 million. This amount was leveraged into $3.2 billion, an extraordinary 13-to-1 leverage ratio. The losses were then shifted by transferring bonds at "book value," that is, face value, rather than at market value. The biggest transfer took place November 1, when the Treasurer's office shifted some $2 billion from fund 100 to the Orange County commingled fund. By the time the pool collapsed, Number 100 was empty.

Citron's lawyer argued that, because the bonds were intended to be held to maturity, "there was no loss" when the transfers took place. Why the transfers were necessary at all was not discussed. Acting Treasurer Thomas Daxon immediately put all 14 remaining employees in his office on leave; while careful not to impute blame, Daxon made it clear that his intention was to reassure outsiders of the integrity of the Treasurer's office. Overall, the disclosure of the transfer increased the share of losses to the county by about 5% and decreased those of participants by about 3%.

There were other questionable shifts and transfers. In 1993, the city of Laguna Beach was devastated by fire. To help provide funds for reconstruction, Robert Citron engineered a deal whereby the city of Laguna Beach invested $1 million in a fund that was leveraged into $50 million worth of securities. Citron promised to take back the securities at face value, thus guaranteeing safety of principal. Laguna Beach took a profit of $1.5 million from this arrangement just three weeks before the bankruptcy. The value of the securities, however, had declined by $12 million, which was transferred to the rest of the investment pool. It goes without saying that Laguna Beach officials have been guarded in their comments on the Orange County crisis.

In other instances, too, Robert Citron appears to have operated as if he felt the funds under his management were his to do with as he wished. As a sort of godfather cum Robin

Hood, he directed revenues to needy causes he himself identified. He never pocketed the public monies, as far as anyone could establish, but there can be no doubt he took great satisfaction in his role as benefactor and munificent savior. As he wrote in his last annual report to the Supervisors:

· ·

We are proud to know that in some way we have assisted local governments in maintaining their level and quality of services. Investment earnings allow educational districts to continue to provide necessary programs to students, and has [sic] allowed cities and the County to better manage the decreasing financial support from the State. To be able to have such a beneficial impact on the citizens of Orange County is extremely satisfying to me, and more importantly to my remarkably professional Treasury staff.

· ·

The county now has to deal with a $1.7 billion loss.

14

Fallout in the County

· ·

"The victims will be our school children with even less funding; residents waiting longer for infrastructure improvements; road users tolerating poor driving conditions due to further delayed maintenance."

JOHN MOORLACH, LETTER TO THE BOARD OF SUPERVISORS
MAY 31, 1994

· ·

The voters of Orange County re-elected Robert Citron without realizing they were signing a blank check—a check worth almost $2 billion.

Without any question, responsibility for the bankruptcy has been widely attributed to Citron and other figures in county government, who are viewed as having betrayed the public trust by their carelessness and indifference. But the lack of supervision given Citron was but a particular instance of a general indifference toward, and disaffection from, local government. Few citizens, for example, know the functions of a county government (as distinct from a state or city authority). The Supervisors who thought of county government

Table 14.1

Participants in the Orange County Pool, November 30, 1994

Participant	Amount ($ million)
County of Orange	2,761
OC Transportation Authority	1,093
OC Sanitation District	441
Transportation corridor agencies	342
OC Employee Retirement System	133
School districts (60 total)	1,048
Cities (37 total)	1,043
Water districts (11 total)	516
Other	41
Total	7,418

as "If it ain't broke, don't fix it," differed only in their power and prominence from the voters who thought, "If it works and I don't have to pay high taxes, vote it in again."

Unfortunately, OCIP's loss was real. It must now be allocated among the various pool participants. The county has already begun to cope with its altered fiscal profile—and it will continue coping for a long time.

Allocating the Losses

All of those who benefited from OCIP's many successful years of operation, and this includes just about everybody in the county, have had to share in its losses, too. Table 14.1 breaks down the amount invested by the various member agencies.

The county initially contended that every participant should share equally in the loss. But this ignored the fact that some participants had been forced to invest in the pool, whereas others did so voluntarily. And only the Supervisors had oversight authority, whether or not they used it. The pool-participants can be divided into three classes:

1. Non-Risk Takers. These are school districts that were forced to invest their idle funds, special districts or agencies whose funds were required by law to be held in trust, and individuals encouraged to place court awards in the pool. They were not merely seeking higher returns but had no choice where to invest.

2. Risk Takers. These made an active choice to be involved with OCIP. This class includes buyers of debt issued by the county and participants in the pool who invested to generate higher returns, such as the cities of Santa Barbara and Claremont.

3. Residual Claimants. This class consists exclusively of the county itself. Not only did the county seek higher returns, it had supervisory responsibility for the treasurer's behavior.

In corporate filings, there is a clear pecking order for creditors. But in municipal bankruptcies, the question of who bears a loss is insufficiently defined by law. Some participants in OCIP claimed that the county, acting as trustee for the pool assets, did not act prudently; and that they (the participants) should therefore be repaid in full ahead of the county. The county, understandably enough, argued that, because investors benefited from the fund's higher returns, they should reasonably expect to bear the losses also.

Two months after the bankruptcy, the Orange County Business Council, a group of local business executives, proposed a settlement plan. To go into effect, the plan had to be approved by 80% of the investors holding at least 90% of the pool's investments. County officials, acting on this plan, offered to repay 77 cents on the dollar to all pool participants. The plan also made the following provision: schools would additionally receive 13 cents in marketable 15-year notes, plus 10 cents in IOUs (a promise to repay, "I owe you"); cities and special districts would receive 3 cents in marketable notes, plus 20 cents in IOUs. The marketable notes were promised to be "as good as gold" and would be "senior" (i.e., be paid first) to other obligations of the county. Holders of the IOUs would have to wait in line with all county creditors.

Pool investors have been presented with two alternatives: Option A, where investors accept the plan but promise not to sue the county and Option B, where investors take only the 77 cents payment but reserve the right to sue. More than 200 OCIP investors chose Option A, agreeing not to sue the county. Some two dozen agencies preferred to reserve the right to sue. On May 19, $2.2 billion were handed out to pool investors. Some of the checks were flown by helicopter to Los Angeles to be deposited before the weekend. The funds will be managed internally or handed out to external money managers. Ideally, agencies will have learned a lesson in risk management.

Reforming the County Budget

The county's share of losses was initially estimated at $510 million. Later, as improper fund transfers came to light, the county's share was put at $800 million. (Both figures are based on an equal allocation of losses in proportion to the monies invested.) The burning issue is, how will the county cope with this loss?

Table 14.2 compares the actual 1993-94 budget and the proposed 1994–95 budget. The county's total budget amounted to about $2.1 billion in the latest fiscal year. Of the total general fund budget, the majority of funds come from state and federal governments, with specific requirements on

Table 14.2

County Budget ($ millions)

Revenues	1993–94	1994–95	Expenses	1993–94	1994–95
Property taxes	218	174	General	212	259
Other taxes	64	18	Public protection	657	749
Permits	12	12	Ways and facilities	90	218
Fines	23	40	Health	226	236
Interest	221	219	Public assistance	520	602
Government	980	1071	Education	23	28
Charges	247	282	Recreation	5	8
Other financing	142	152	Debt service	27	53
Transfers	4	9	Miscellaneous	104	82
Miscellaneous	70	146	Reserves	155	40
Total	1981	2123		2018	2276

Source: Orange County Budget, with 1994–95 as "proposed budget."

how they must be spent. The county's contribution to the general fund—its discretionary spending—was $462 million in 1993-94. This was funded by $221 million from interest revenues (10% of the total). This last figure represented the 8% interest on the $2.8 billion invested in OCIP. Thus, the county had been, and planned to continue to be, living off its interest earnings to a considerable extent.

Most of these interest earnings were now gone. The county estimated its loss of such earnings at $172 million for the first half of 1995 alone. In addition, the county faced a debt bill of about $1.6 billion: $382 million to repay bonds coming due later in 1995; $255 million for the settlement notes; and $924 million for the IOUs under the settlement plan. The county began to address this debt burden by cutting costs. It laid off some 400 workers in January, with another 300 eliminated through retirement and hiring freezes.

Later, another 1,040 lost their jobs. Before these cuts, the county had employed more than 17,000 people, with a total annual personnel bill of around $935 million. By March, the discretionary budget had been sliced from $462 million to $275 million, a drastic 41% cut.

Other proposals for cutting expenses focused on delaying or halting some public projects and on contracting out or privatizing government services. Even though a very wealthy county by any standard (total population, 2.6 million), Orange County includes over 400,000 people who depend on welfare to some extent and about 15,000 homeless. The first wave of cuts in services had a great impact on such people by targeting the county bus system, nutrition programs for the homeless, children's health care and other welfare services, and legal services for the poor.

Certain political elements in the county argued that the bankruptcy was an opportunity for changing the structure of government in a permanent way. The Committees of Correspondence, for example—a local coalition of Howard Jarvis-style tax protesters and followers of Ross Perot's United We Stand America—began a public campaign centered around a slogan of "No tax increase, no bailout, downsize government!" The *Orange County Register*, the major local daily paper, similarly called the bankruptcy a "wonderful opportunity" while urging the Board of Supervisors to drive down wages and permanently curb the influence of the county unions.

Taxes are an important issue everywhere, and the prospect of raising taxes went to the very heart of Orange County's dilemma. If we can see that undue reliance on Citron's investments grew directly from passage of Proposition 13, which severely limited property tax revenues available to local governments, we begin to understand the (painful) irony of the adamant opposition to new taxes that followed the bankruptcy. Yet Orange County, like other governmental bodies issuing debt, was on record as having put its "full faith and credit" behind the bonds it purveyed. This meant—if it meant anything—that the county was pledged to use its taxing power when necessary.

Raising property taxes seemed an impossibility; notwithstanding the political difficulties, Proposition 13 requires a two-thirds electoral approval for any change in tax rates. (Higher property taxes might have been the most rational approach, however; property taxes are deductible against federal income taxes, thus they benefit from a tax subsidy from the federal government.) Raising sales taxes seemed more likely, at least in theory. The sales tax in Los Angeles County is 8.25%; in San Francisco County, 8.5%; but in Orange County, only 7.75%. An increase of half a cent would generate about $140 million a year for the county, at a cost of about $50 per resident. (The value of this tax, if kept in place forever and assuming a 4% rate of interest, can be computed from the stream of future payments. Because these would go up with the rate of inflation, the appropriate discount rate is the *real* rate of interest. This yields $140/0.04 = $3,500 million. More than enough to cover a $1.7 billion loss.)

The simple mention of new taxes, though, raises political firestorms in Orange County. The Supervisors, when they endorsed the rescue plan in February, made clear their strong opposition to new taxes, to widespread approval. By April, however, the realities of the debt situation had led them to take a previously unthinkable step: they placed a measure on the June ballot to raise the sales tax to 8.25%. (As this book was being written, that campaign was in progress and the outcome in doubt, though most polls showed the tax proposal headed for defeat.)

In lieu of new taxes, the county considered selling off some of its assets, such as John Wayne Airport. As a general rule, the sale of public assets is a good idea only if the need for cash is so great as to override other considerations or if the private sector is likely to operate the asset more efficiently. John Wayne Airport brought in about $40 million a year in profits to the county, which bespeaks a reasonably efficient operation. Discounting the profits at the current real rate of interest of 4%, the fair value of the airport would be $40/0.04 = $1,000 million. But selling an asset simply transforms the future stream of profits into a cash payment now. The county forfeits future revenues, and in any case, an airport is unlikely to sell in a hurry.

All things being equal, fiscal health for Orange County appeared to require, not the desperate sale of assets, but careful, sensible expense cutting and some new taxes (if only the voters and politicians would allow). Absent a successful effort to deal with the debt, the county stands to suffer serious and perhaps permanent consequences: as we have seen, an outright default (for example, on the notes coming due in the summer of 1995) would have meant much higher costs on any future borrowing. Equally important, default would have had a negative effect on property values in the county. Home buyers for many years had come to Orange County because of its schools (generally perceived to be better than those in nearby Los Angeles County). As we can see from Box 14.1, however, the crisis had serious consequences for the local school districts.

Real estate values and sales were both down following the bankruptcy; many transactions in progress at the time were canceled. Consider the situation of an imaginary family planning to buy a house in Irvine, a city made attractive by the high quality of its schools. Now programs were to be cut, teachers and administrators fired en masse, and parents required to serve as custodians. One way or another, county residents will have to pay for the bankruptcy.

Box 14.1

The Irvine Unified School District was particularly affected by OCIP's losses. Irvine had invested $105 million in OCIP, the most of any school system. Irvine's schools had consistently been ranked among the top in California, and Irvine High School was considered one of the best public schools in the nation. But under the pay-out plan proposed in February, the Irvine district stood to lose as much as $10 million, or 10% of its operating budget.

The district circulated a questionnaire to Irvine residents asking them where cuts should be directed. The School Board identified $3 million in cuts, which would result in the elimination of 120 teaching jobs, the consolidation of summer programs, and substantially reduced administrative staff.

There was some support for a temporary "parcel tax" (requiring approval of two-thirds of voters). A parcel tax of $105 per annum would have covered the $3 million budget shortfall. Failing passage of the tax, deep cuts would take place; parents would need to donate pencils, paper, and other supplies to schools and to perform what were described as "light janitorial services."

15

Lessons in Risk

. . . .

The financial disaster in Orange County led to calls for government action. What is to be done? Should investment pools be prohibited from investing in any type of risky asset? Should the derivatives markets be closed, or some portions thereof? Should the government issue stricter regulations guiding the relationship between brokers and municipalities? Should we force greater disclosure from municipalities to investors and bondholders? Should we revisit the role of federal agencies as issuers of securities?

Setting Objectives

First, we must recall that *all financial investments are risky, for there would be no reward without risk.* The issue is the amount of risk investors are willing to stomach. The $1.7 billion loss in Orange County represents a fall of 22% in a $7.5 billion investment pool. To put things in perspective, a passive investment with the average maturity of the Treasury market would have lost only about 4% of its value in 1994. OCIP's abnormally large loss reflects the high degree of leverage of the portfolio, which exacerbated market risk.

This high degree of market risk was due to two factors. First, the fund's manager implemented speculative positions with substantial downside risk, which were inconsistent with the responsibilities of running a public fund. Through investments in agency and structured notes and leverage, OCIP was betting on stable or falling rates. Essentially, the pool operated as a "hedge" fund, such as those run by George Soros, which would have brought substantial rewards if rates moved in the hoped-for direction. But hedge funds put capital at substantial risk.

Second, OCIP suffered from a convenient failure of controls. Investors who benefited from OCIP's extraordinary performance over previous years might well have suspected that the fund's strategy was unusually risky. How else had OCIP been able to outperform the industry average? Participants in the pool profited from this superior performance, yet turned a blind eye to risks.

Investors ignored a fundamental principle of finance: higher returns are inevitably related to higher risks. Figure 15.1 displays the risk and return of five assets classes: cash, medium-term notes, long-term bonds, and large and small stocks. Clearly, higher returns came only at the expense of higher risks over the last 50 years. As the display demonstrates, small stocks returned 16% annually, but with a volatility of 20%. Large stocks were safer, with a volatility of 14%, but returned less, 12%. Cash was safe but returned only 5%. Higher returns, higher risk.

When shareholders invest in a private corporation, they put their own capital at risk, and they may willingly accept a speculative investment strategy by the company. But the contributors to public funds are acting on behalf of taxpayers

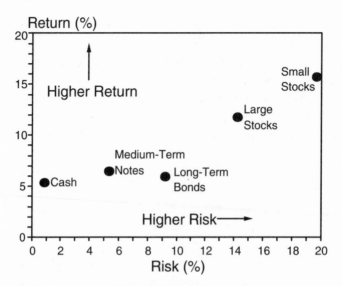

Figure 15.1 Higher Return, Higher Risk

and their families, and they need to set clear investment objectives for the portfolio. If the portfolio is subject to large and frequent cash withdrawals (because of the cash-flow needs of participating bodies), then it should be invested in very short-term securities and have preservation of principal as its first objective. Conversely, if the funds are used mainly to generate interest revenues and can be left in a pool for some years, the portfolio can expose itself to more risk and longer maturities in hopes of gaining higher returns.

If funds are invested long term, they can be used to create a "financial hedge" against variations in a government's tax revenues. Assume, for example, that revenues fluctuate over the years as a function of business activity. (This has especially been the case in California, which with Proposition 13 shifted tax revenues away from relatively stable property taxes toward less predictable income and sales taxes.) Assets that increase in value during recessions, when tax revenues decline, offer a buffer against shortfalls. This provides a rationale for investing in longer term bonds, for example.

Once the objectives of the fund are clearly delineated, they can be translated into guidelines for a *risk management system*. This sets limits on market exposure in view of cash-flow needs and so forth. Consider, as an example, the "value at risk" system that follows.

Controlling Risk

Every morning, Jim Garnett, the senior vice president in charge of global risk management at Chase Manhattan Bank, receives a 30-page report summarizing the "value at risk" (VAR) of the bank. This document is generated during the night by computers that quantify the risk of the bank's many trading positions.

What is a VAR? It is a summary of *the worst possible losses over a target horizon within a given confidence interval.* Or more simply, the worst losses to expect in a given period and how likely they are. For example, let us go back to Figure 3.4, which describes the monthly returns (price changes) of different bonds over the last 50 years. For medium-term notes, returns ranged from a low of −6.5% to a high of +12.0%. Now construct regularly spaced "bins" going from the lowest to the highest number, and count how many observations fall into each bin. For instance, there is one observation below −5%. There is another observation between −5% and −4.5%. And so on. In this way, we construct a probability distribution for the monthly returns, which counts how many occurrences have been observed in the past for a particular range. Such a distribution is represented in Figure 15.2.

For each return, one can compute a probability of observing a lower return. Pick a confidence level, say 5%. This

Number of Occurrences

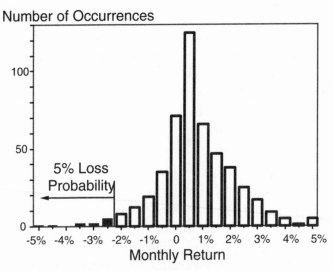

Figure 15.2 Measuring Value at Risk (VAR)

represents the worst possible outcome over a month. For each confidence level, one can find on the graph a point such that there is a 5% probability of finding a lower return. From Figure 15.2, this number is −2%. This is because all occurrences of returns less than −2% add up to 5% of the total number of months.

We can now compute the VAR of a $100 million portfolio. There is only a 5% chance that the portfolio value will fall by more than $100 million times 2%, or $2 million. Therefore, the value at risk is $2 million. Under normal market conditions, the most one can lose is $2 million over a month.

Note that this number is directly related to the concept of duration. As we know from a previous chapter, we arrive at the dollar loss by multiplying duration by the increase in yield. Assume a duration of four years for this investment. If the worst increase in yields over a month, at the 5% level, is 0.5%, then the worst loss is given by

Worst Dollar Loss	=	Duration	×	Dollar Portfolio Value	×	Worst Yield Increase
	=	4 Years	×	$100m	×	0.5%

which is also $2 million! Therefore the value at risk is directly related to the concept of duration.

But the VAR approach is more general; it allows investors to include many assets, such as foreign currencies, commodities, and equities. It can also account for interest rate movements that differ across maturities.

The VAR approach is fast gaining acceptance as the swiftest method for measuring market risks. With the falling costs of computing power and widely available software to measure VAR, there simply is no excuse for not using this system.

Many banks, brokerage firms, and mutual funds already gauge their market exposure this way. Regulators and central banks, in their quest to control the "derivatives monster," now lean toward forcing financial institutions to reveal their VAR. (Regulators can force implementation because they can set capital adequacy requirements based on a bank's VAR.)

These concepts, as complex as they seem at first, actually simplify communications with nontechnical audiences. For example, the state auditor reported that in November 1994, the interest rate exposure of the fund was such that, for every point (percent) increase in interest rates, the portfolio stood to lose $560 million. These numbers explained the fund's exposure in a clear and useful way.

If Robert Citron had made similar presentations of market risk, investors might have thought more carefully about what they were doing with their money.

Risk and Derivatives

· ·

Although derivatives have come under recent attack as being inherently risky, their essential function is providing a market for the *exchange of financial risks.* To illustrate, it may be useful to view derivatives in the context of historical developments.

A Brief History of Derivatives

The earliest known form of financial agreement was a loan. Say a farmer wished to plant more crops. Lacking sufficient resources himself, he sought out a lender, and with the capital he borrowed, he bought seed and tools and access to acreage. A loan of this kind allowed more efficient use of available resources, and it also *made both parties subject to the risk of crop failure.* This risk-spreading feature of the loan was crucial to economic dynamism.

In ancient Babylonia, caravans were the primary means of trade. Investors provided capital to traders, who bought goods to sell and outfitted their caravans. To help manage the risk of robbery, the Babylonians devised a system of contracts in which investors supplied capital, yet agreed to cancel loans if the traders were robbed of their goods. The trader who took out this kind of loan paid an extra amount—a premium—for having such protection. (This is also like buying an "option" to cancel a loan.) As for the lender, collecting a premium from many traders made it possible to absorb the losses of the unlucky few.

Bonds and equities developed in the 16th century. The Amsterdam Stock Exchange (opened 1611) was the first true market for bonds and other kinds of securities. "Time bargains"—primitive options and futures—were soon being traded there.

In Japan, futures trading goes back to 1730, when the Dojima Rice Market came into being. The Dojima's purpose was to protect planters from price fluctuations between harvests, and it brought an important element of stability.

In the United States, commodities futures exchanges emerged in Chicago and New York. The Chicago Board of Trade (CBOT) was established in 1848 to set quality standards for grain contracts, but soon it was functioning as the premises for an active trade in agricultural futures.

An important innovation of the CBOT was the idea of *offsetting* contracts. Traders were relieved of the obligation of actually delivering the grain and other goods they dealt in; they freed themselves of these obligations by selling contracts they had purchased previously (or by buying an equal number of opposite contracts, marked for the same delivery month). The ability to *offset* provided impetus to the trade in futures in and of themselves.

In the 1970s, an era of markedly increased volatility in interest rates and exchange rates, the Chicago exchanges presented other innovations. For instance, they inaugurated *futures trading on financial instruments* (such as bonds and mortgages) and *stock options*.

The exchange markets have developed efficient mechanisms to protect against customer defaults in derivatives trading. In addition to requiring margin deposits, all contracts are *marked-to-market*. This entails the daily settling of gains and losses and prevents situations where traders accumulate large losses they are not able to cover.

Consider that a type of derivative instrument, Treasury note futures, which are commonly traded on the CBOT, can be used to hedge (protect against) interest rate exposure. By mid-December 1994, OCIP's exposure was such that, for every 1% rise in rates, the fund stood to lose $300 million. This exposure could have been hedged by going short (agreeing to sell) about 800 contracts in the 5-year T note futures market.

Date	Portfolio Loss	Futures Price	Futures Gain	Total Loss
December 1994		100.00		
January 1995	−$300m	96.25	+$300m	$0

Say that the futures price was originally quoted at 100. Assume that interest rates indeed went up by 1%. Remember, increasing rates lead to falling bond prices; therefore, the futures contract also falls, say to 96.25. Because the position is short, this leads to a gain of 800 contracts times the face value of a contract ($100,000) times the change in the futures price, or $3.75. The profit is

$$800 \times \$100,000 \times (100 - 96.25) = \$300 \text{ million},$$

which is a perfect offset to the portfolio loss.

In other words, had Robert Citron wanted to hedge, or speculate on, interest rates, he could have done so by taking positions in interest rate futures, rather than by investing questionably in repos and structured notes. Taking positions in futures contracts would have had many advantages; for one, transactions in competitive markets tend to occur at fair prices. For another, should liquidation have become necessary, the process would have been far simpler.

For Citron, however—and possibly also for the brokers who sold structured notes to the OCIP and made handsome commissions from them—the exchange markets must have been oddly unattractive. They would have invited a close scrutiny and a regular reckoning of gains and losses (remember marking to market). Furthermore, using futures would have defeated Citron's grand strategy of "holding to maturity." But, as we have seen, losses exist whether totted up or not.

Derivatives as Risk Management Tools

Do derivatives serve a useful social function? Or are they fundamentally instruments of dangerous speculation?

The answer is, it depends. Derivatives when used unwisely can certainly lead to catastrophe. But derivatives are innovations in *risk management*, not in risk itself. *Risk exists because there is uncertainty in the world.* To equate derivatives with pointless speculation, or with pure gambling, is certainly wrong: gambling entails the creation of *new* risks (as in games like roulette or poker).

Speculation, for that matter, means engagement with *pre-existing* risks (such as droughts, earthquakes, exchange rate movements and inflation). Speculation is more correctly seen as a necessary counterpart to hedging, and hedging itself is a means by which individuals (or businesses, or countries) seek protection against changes over which they have no control. Hedging assumes the existence of speculators, who are entities willing to take speculative counterpositions—and who, in their (one hopes efficient) search for profits, provide important liquidity to markets.

But, as shown in Box 16.1, investing in derivatives can also be an entirely prudent exercise, as well as a highly profitable one.

Box 16.1 PIMCO's Approach to Derivatives

Pacific Investment Management (PIMCO), based in Newport Beach, in Orange County, is a leading fixed-income asset manager. Now with over $55 billion under its control, PIMCO has used the derivative markets since 1980, when it first began taking positions in financial futures.

PIMCO is a pension fund manager among other things, and as such, its policies are subject to strict guidelines designed to protect the interests of pension beneficiaries. In a typical transaction, PIMCO compares the value of investing in bonds directly or indirectly through financial futures, choosing the cheaper alternative. Over the past 10 years PIMCO has shown returns exceeding its benchmark portfolio by 1.3% annually. Its investment style is careful, incremental, and effective.

Not to underplay the risks of speculation in derivatives, Table 16.1 displays some recent spectacular losses over the last two years alone.

To focus on these losses alone, however, is misleading for three reasons. First, derivatives positions were taken in some, but certainly not all, situations as a hedge; that is, to offset other business risks. Thus the losses may be offset by operating profits. (It has been argued, for instance, that the Metallgesellschaft losses were partially offset by increases in the value of oil contracts with customers.)

Second, the size of these losses is directly related to recent large movements in financial markets. In 1994 alone,

Table 16.1

Losses Attributed to Derivatives: 1993–94

	Instrument	Loss ($ million)
Showa Shell Sekiyu	Currency forwards	1,580
Kashima Oil	Currency derivatives	1,450
Metallgesellschaft	Oil futures	1,340
Codelco, Chile	Copper futures	200
Procter & Gamble	Structured notes	157
Minnetonka Fund	Mortgage derivatives	90
Dell Computer	Leveraged swaps	34
Gibson Greetings	Leveraged swaps	23
ARCO Pension Fund	Structured notes	22

Source: Capital Market Risk Advisors.

interest rate movements created losses for holders of U.S. Treasury bonds (supposedly "safe" investments) of about *$230 billion.*

Third, these derivatives losses were gains to a number of other individuals or institutions. (Winners usually complain less than losers.) These markets can even be favorable to neophytes, especially if the investors are well-advised. A notable example is Hillary Clinton, who, according to documents released in connection with the Whitewater investigation, parlayed $1,000 into $100,000 in commodity futures trades between 1978 and 1980.

Monitoring Risks

In 1993, the Group of Thirty (G30), a respected industry association, conducted a thorough review of the OTC derivatives markets. It examined the risks associated with derivative products and concluded that derivatives introduce risks of no greater scale than those *already* present in financial markets. The G30 report also provided a set of sound management guidelines, which can be summarized as follows:

1. Determine at the highest level of decision making whether to trade in derivatives. In other words, let top management define the proper scope of involvement (not some less responsible or authoritative individual).
2. Value derivative positions at market prices; that is, check the profits and losses every day.
3. Quantify market risk under adverse conditions and perform stress simulations (i.e., think of what might happen in an untoward market situation, in view of fund limits).
4. Assess the credit risk arising from derivatives activities (i.e., check whether a counterparty might default).
5. Establish market and credit risk functions with clear authority, independent of the dealing function (i.e., make sure trading activity is supervised).
6. Authorize only professionals with the necessary skills and experience to transact (i.e., make sure traders are qualified).

These standards of the G30 are not only sensible and straightforward, they can be applied to any type of portfolio, in derivatives or other kinds of markets.

With standards such as these in place, an investment manager has a more than reasonable chance of avoiding an OCIP-style debacle. The rules, however, should not be so rigidly enforced as to paralyze investment decisions; managers need the freedom to navigate effectively *within* the rules. The Municipal Treasurers Association has suggested use of the "prudent man's" standard in investment decisions, according to the following formula:

. . . .

Investment officers acting in accordance with written procedures and investment policy and exercising the diligence that is appropriate, shall be relieved of personal responsibility for an individual security credit risk or market price changes, provided deviations from expectations are reported in a timely fashion and appropriate action is taken to control adverse developments.

. . . .

To sum up, once the parameters of risk are defined and oversight mechanisms put in place, derivatives present no special threat to investment managers. Indeed, derivatives are highly useful for investors when used prudently.

Unhappy outcomes, such as OCIP's collapse, are often associated with inattention to market risk. For example, OCIP was restricted by charter to investing in obligations of the U.S. government, notes of its agencies, and investment-grade corporate debt. Such restrictions, typical of those established by politicians, are overly concerned with minimizing credit risk. The investment guidelines of the OCIP only emphasized *safety* (as measured by credit risk), *liquidity*, and *yield*, in that order. But, as we have seen, long-term Treasuries or structured agency notes can be extremely exposed to market risk. And market risk of a high enough order can lead to default.

In today's continually evolving markets, the control environment just described, defined largely in terms of market risk, is the best approach to investment management. Financial innovations will always be one step ahead of state investment guidelines. The only safeguard against dangerous mistakes is understanding all sources of risk.

A Lesson (Leeson) in Risk: the Fall of Barings Bank

On February 26, 1995, the Queen of Great Britain woke up to the news that Barings PLC, a venerable 233-year-old

English institution, had gone bankrupt. It appeared that a single trader, 28-year-old Nicholas Leeson, had lost more than $1.4 billion in derivatives trades. The bank that defeated Napoleon's armies had succumbed to a single rogue trader—and to that wild beast, the *derivative.*

The loss came mainly from exposure to the Japanese stock market, achieved through futures trading. Leeson had been accumulating positions in stock index futures on the Nikkei 225 (a portfolio of Japanese stocks). Barings's total positions on the Singapore and Osaka exchanges added up to a staggering $7 billion. As the market fell 15% in the first two months of 1995, Barings Futures Singapore, of which Leeson was chief trader, suffered huge losses that were made even worse by the sale of options. (These sales had been used to generate cash to fund the losing positions in futures.) As losses mounted, Leeson stubbornly increased the size of his position. Then, unable to make the cash payments required by the exchanges, he simply walked away. Later he sent a fax to his superiors, offering "sincere apologies for the predicament that I have left you in."

Because Barings was viewed as a conservative bank, the affair served as a wake-up call for financial institutions all over the world. It revealed an amazing lack of supervision at Barings: Leeson had control over both the trading desk and the "back office," which confirms trades and checks that all activity is within guidelines. In a well-run bank, traders have a limited amount of capital to play with, and they are subject to "position limits" verified by the back office. Mixing the trading and back office functions is like giving a child a checkbook and also allowing it to balance the books. The temptation to cheat can be overwhelming.

Furthermore, most banks now have a separate risk-management unit that provides another check on traders. Sensible risk-management guidelines, as we have seen, have been clearly spelled out, as in the Group of Thirty report of 1993.

By one estimate, Barings had ignored half of the best practices recommendations from G30.

The Singapore and Osaka exchanges also drew attention for failing to notice the size of Leeson's positions. On each exchange, Barings Futures had accumulated a position of $3.5 billion, about 10 times the size of the next largest position. Officials at U.S. futures exchanges declared that such positions would have attracted their attention much sooner. (One only hopes so.) The situation was an embarrassment for Singapore, which has been trying to position itself as "one of the most sound and secure marketplaces in the world."

Singapore is also known for its harsh criminal sentencing practices, as witnessed by the caning of an American student convicted of spray-painting cars in 1994. No wonder Leeson promptly left Singapore. Since his arrest in Germany, he has been vigorously fighting extradition to Singapore.

Leeson, like Robert Citron, was allowed to run free largely because of his track record. In 1994, Leeson made about $20 million for Barings, or about one-fifth the firm's total profits. This translated into fat bonuses for Leeson and his superiors. The head of Barings Securities, Christopher Heath, was Britain's highest paid executive during this period. Leeson could place market bets of almost any size because he was viewed as a hero, just like Citron.

Barings apparently ignored an internal audit, drawn up in 1994, that warned of "excessive concentration of power" in Leeson's hands. There were also allegations that senior bank executives, aware of the risks he was taking, had approved cash transfers of $1 billion to make margin calls.

In both the Orange County and Barings fiascos, a lone manager speculated and lost—heavily. Neither Citron nor Leeson had the courage to admit his mistakes and then cut his losses. But in both cases, the lack of internal supervision was so extreme that it seems fanciful, or anyhow superficial, to try to lay the blame on the type of instruments being traded.

The price of Barings's shares went to zero, wiping out about $1 billion of market capitalization. Bondholders received 5 cents on the dollar (5 pence on the pound). Some of the additional losses were borne by the Dutch financial-services group International Nederlanden Group (ING), which offered to acquire Barings for the grand total of one British pound—about $1.50.

17

Do We Need Regulation?

* *

"Regulation is not meant to insulate investors from the consequences of free economic forces, or from their own poor judgment, but rather from abuses perpetrated by other persons."

PHILIP M. JOHNSON, FORMER CHAIR
COMMODITIES FUTURES TRADING COMMISSION

* *

The Orange County fiasco has inevitably led to calls for tighter regulation of financial markets. In general, regulation is considered necessary when the market fails in either of two respects: through excessive prices or through opportunistic behavior.

In a free market, with adequately informed customers, prices can be excessive only if sellers collude to maintain high prices. Antitrust legislation, such as the Sherman Act of 1890, was designed to prevent such collusion.

Opportunistic behavior can arise because of access to inside information, which puts informed sellers at an advantage over buyers. Trading on inside information is prohibited in U.S. markets. Another species of opportunistic behavior is the feeding of false information to clients, who then trade on it.

These two classic motives for regulation fail to apply to the Orange County affair, at least in any obvious way. Robert Citron had access to many brokers, who appear not to have colluded as regards prices. Nor is there evidence that any of OCIP's brokers withheld material information to Citron, although they may have been self-serving—or just wrong—in their predictions about interest rate movements.

In 1994, a Cincinnati paper company, Gibson Greetings, lost some $20 million on derivatives trades. But the Gibson case, unlike Orange County's, involved documented illegal behavior on the part of brokers. Gibson entered into complex derivatives contracts with Bankers Trust, an investment bank, starting in 1991. Initially, these contracts generated large profits and Gibson did not complain (but somebody else lost money). Starting in 1994, however, the fatidic interest rate hikes that felled Citron turned these profits into large losses. The company was relying on the bank's valuation model to make decisions, but some brokers at the bank gave Gibson false information, hiding $6 million dollars in losses. Gibson then entered into additional trades, which led to further losses. For such opportunistic behavior, Bankers Trust was sanctioned by regulatory agencies and fined $10 million.

Whenever catastrophes occur, there is a natural tendency to consider new regulations. In response to Orange County, state legislators have proposed laws deeming local governments "unsophisticated investors." (Robert Citron, after 24 years in the Treasurer's office, would thus become a financial babe in arms.) New regulations are satisfying to impose, but they sometimes have unpleasant consequences. Nor are they always needed. In the wake of OCIP's experience, for example, government officials across the country have already begun to examine their investment policies with a new thoroughness and seriousness. Orange County has served, willy-nilly, as a powerful object lesson in the need for strict and continuous oversight and a clear risk management policy.

Regulation is often costly. For example, if fund managers are called unsophisticated investors and municipalities find it easier to sue, brokers will pass their penalty and court costs along to their customers, the investors. As a former SEC commissioner put it, "Someone has to pay for the extra insurance and . . . liability, even for the times the totally honest professional is accused because his client lost money."

Legislators have also floated proposals to prohibit all derivatives trading in public investments. Such regulations, if actually put in effect, would be almost impossible to enforce: derivatives, as we have seen, are "hidden" in many ordinary-looking securities. For example, callable bonds, which can be called back from buyers if interest rates fall, involve a short position in an option; many Treasury and agency bonds are callable. The innocuous-looking savings bonds also contain embedded options. Derivatives may also be evolving too rapidly in the current financial environment for reform-minded officials to keep up with them. By the time reforms are proposed, discussed, written as legislation, and approved, new forms of financial products have appeared.

The best approach, then, is to require clearly stated investment guidelines, a risk management system for monitoring of developments, and more disclosure to investors. In his last annual report, Robert Citron wrote:

. . . .

Some investment funds regulated by the Securities and Exchange Commission are required to periodically adjust the cost of their portfolios to reflect current market values which may result in a paper gain or loss. Government accounting standards do not require municipal investment pools to make this periodic adjustment. Therefore, we are not required to record "paper" gains or losses.

. . . .

But regular, detailed disclosure might have saved Citron even from himself. If OCIP's holdings had been made public every month, for example, and measured at current market values, the treasurer might have recognized just how risky his investments actually were. Investors, in touch with monthly fluctuations in values, might also have refrained from the "run on the bank" that happened in December. (The run was because investors could pull out their money at 100 cents on the dollar, while the value of the underlying assets was insufficient to cover such a sum. Marking to market would have removed, or at least lessened, the incentive to withdraw funds ahead of other investors because it would have provided an ongoing, realistic image of portfolio value.)

The need for disclosure should be considered in the context of recent trends in financial markets. The problem with classic financial accounting in the current environment is that balance sheets report assets and liabilities only. Fifty years ago, when instruments were quite simple, this was probably adequate; but a five-year structured note, to take an example, may have a positive, zero, or negative exposure to interest rates. Thus to report its maturity, as a balance sheet would do, is meaningless. Also, derivative contracts such as forwards and swaps simply do not appear on balance sheets—thus some very essential information remains hidden.

Whenever catastrophes occur, there is always a tendency to blame the instrument used and to ask for reform. But blanket regulation is rarely wise—as history teaches us, you cannot legislate common sense.

The Problem with Structured Notes

Some of OCIP's losses can be traced to inappropriate use of these complicated products. Structured notes, as you will recall, are issued by agencies of the federal government, and they typically contain "embedded" derivatives.

There are two main problems with structured notes. The first is that they may be *overpriced*. Structured notes are customized to the borrower's or investor's needs and typically involve unique features that make them difficult to price. This situation is opposite to that on organized exchanges, which deal in derivatives, which are *easy* to price, and where a competitive market exists, thus ensuring *fair* pricing.

The high prices at which structured notes sometimes sell mean lower funding costs for borrowers. Helped with government implicit guarantees, U.S. government agencies are massive borrowers; their outstanding debt is second only to that of the U.S. Treasury. Of this agency debt, almost 20%, or over $100 billion, is in structured notes.

Structured notes also generate fat profits for brokers. In many cases, a bank designs the notes, then persuades an agency to issue them, and finally arranges for a client to buy them. In February 1994, for example, Merrill underwrote a $400 million structured note issued by Fannie Mae. Interest was based on a complicated formula pegged to movements in LIBOR. Because of the complexity of the issue, Merrill charged the issuer an underwriting fee four times the size of the usual fee for a fixed-rate note. The Orange County pool then bought the entire issue, perhaps at excessive cost. Bob Citron, however, was not forced into buying this issue from Merrill. In the words of a fellow treasurer, "Bob Citron was not taking orders from anybody."

The second, and more serious, problem with structured notes is that unsophisticated investors may believe they are buying *safe* assets. Many investors, in fact, are restricted by charter to investing in government or agency debt, yet agency debt need not go through the same disclosure requirements as corporate debt. *Structured notes, however, offer patterns of risk and reward similar to those of exchange-listed futures and options.* Funds that are forbidden to speculate in such instruments, because of their supposed risk, often buy structured notes on the basis of their "government security" classification and feel dangerously secure doing so.

Here we can see the perverse effect of certain regulations against derivatives. Such rules can push investors into buying instruments just as risky as listed derivatives, but also overpriced.

Allowing investment funds to deal in exchange-listed futures and options would get around this problem. First, as we have seen, organized exchanges are competitive markets; if a contract has too high a price, many potential sellers immediately appear to bid it down. Second, contracts on organized exchanges are simpler to understand and are valued on a daily basis.

The potential risk of structured notes explains why federal regulators have looked very closely at the purchase of such notes by commercial and savings banks. Depositors at these banks are protected by Federal Deposit Insurance (FDIC). If a bank fails, the government is ultimately liable for the losses (it has granted an "option"). Widespread failures of savings and loans have already cost the government, that is, the taxpayer, about $150 billion. Aware of the government's potential liability, bank examiners have been given the authority to seek the "orderly divestiture" of structured notes.

The Orange County affair directed attention to the agency structured note market and to the implicit government guarantee that most agency debt carries. An unconscious sense that something was wrong may explain why Fannie Mae paid $577 million to buy back a package of seven securities it had sold OCIP. This price was considerably more than what these securities would have fetched on the open market.

If the negative publicity about the structured note market helps to avoid future losses, then the Orange County disaster will have produced another important benefit, albeit rather expensively.

18

Conclusions

· · · · · · · · · · · · · · ·

"Victory has a hundred fathers, but defeat is an orphan."

COUNT GALEAZZO CIANO
DIARY (1946)

· ·

O nce known worldwide as the home of aerospace and Disneyland, Orange County became famous for bankruptcy in December 1994. After having recovered from mudslides, fires, an earthquake, and cuts in defense spending, the county suffered an epidemic of fiscal irresponsibility leading to the largest municipal failure in U.S. history.

Once called a *paper loss*, Orange County's vanished $1.7 billion was undeniably real. It can perhaps be explained most simply in Box 18.1. This loss has already been translated into substantial reductions in services in the county and many lost jobs. There will be no quick fix. No magical deliverance at the hands of some Robert Citron-like "wizard." Bob Citron already granted the county $755 million in free money.

Box 18.1 Summary of the Loss

The $7.5 billion portfolio was invested in bonds with an average maturity of four years, and supercharged by $12.5 billion in short-term loans that were reinvested in bonds. The loss basically stems from an increase in interest rates from 5% to 7% in 1994. As a result, the $20 billion total portfolio was stuck with coupon payments lower than current interest rates. Simplifying to the extreme, we can add the total interest payments over a 4 year horizon. With a 5% coupon, the total interest return is

$$\$20 \text{ billion} \times 5\% \times 4 = \$4,000 \text{ million}.$$

In contrast, a 7% coupon would return a total of $5,600 million. The opportunity loss is therefore $1.6 billion. Whether one holds to maturity or not, the loss is real.

In the end, Orange County will be judged by how it deals with its new situation. Will the county's conservative, tax-hating leaders succeed in convincing the voters that there is indeed no free lunch?

We have seen in this book how exposure to interest rate risk, consistently achieved through various investments, was the primary cause of the $1.7 billion loss. The manager of the Orange County Investment Pool engaged in a systematic policy of betting on falling rates; after years of stable or appreciating bond prices, a reversal in the bond market, as interest rates began rising early in 1994, brought serious consequences for many investors.

Commercial banks, investment banks, hedge funds, corporations, and the supposedly safer investment pools all took substantial hits. The year 1994 humbled many. George Soros, who made profits of $1 billion speculating against the British pound in 1992, lost $600 million in 1994. Leon Cooperman, who started the year with a $3 billion hedge fund, lost $1.2 billion from bad bets on foreign bonds and the peso. Investors and corporations alike have suffered losses due to derivatives. After the fact, many losers have pleaded "financial insanity"—they apparently did not understand the instruments they were dealing with.

There have been calls for restrictions on derivatives trading. In my view, prohibiting all securities that involve derivatives and allowing only investments in "safe" Treasury securities is a seriously misguided policy. The lesson in 1994, for OCIP and others, was that *exposure to market risk always matters. It will be ignored only at an investor's peril.* Treasury securities, as I hope to have demonstrated, can also be dangerous. Investing in a 30-year Treasury bond, for example, which is supposedly safe because backed by the full faith and credit of the U.S. government, would have brought losses of about 12% in 1994.

Many errors flow from focusing on credit risk at the expense of market risk. Strict guidelines will always be one step behind constantly evolving global capital markets. Good judgment cannot be regulated.

Why don't we adopt a simpler rule. *Understand the inherent risks of your investment position and your exposure to these risks, and do not buy any product that you cannot understand or price with reasonable accuracy.* To communicate these risks more effectively, municipal and other investment pools should report the market value of their positions on a regular basis. This provides feedback both to investors and to the portfolio managers, and it eliminates the rationale of a "run on the bank."

A portfolio should also explicitly report its duration (exposure to interest rates). Equivalently, the "value at risk," or maximum monthly loss, is a useful summarization of portfolio risk. As the whole banking system is now moving toward marking to market, so should municipal funds.

Orange County's high-flying plunge may yet prove a cautionary tale for local government and public agencies all over the country. I hope it becomes a lesson to be studied, something to be learned from, in a spirit of compassionate understanding and with a determination not to let this unhappy history repeat.

Epilogue

· · · · · · · · · · · ·

I n late June, 1995, Orange County voters overwhelmingly rejected "Measure R," the proposal to increase the local sales tax by 0.5%. The defeat torpedoed the county's recovery plan, spooking Wall Street and reviving calls for a state takeover.

To outsiders, the vote confirmed the county's reputation as an anti-tax bastion. The New York Times called Orange County a "wealthy deadbeat" unwilling to pay its debt. The fifth largest county in the United States was compared to Russia, Cuba, and China, all notorious for walking away from their obligations.

Inside Orange County, the vote summarized a complex reality. It signaled civic rage against the elected county officials who were all (except Bob Citron) still in office. Voters would not accept the political establishment simply sticking them with the tab. Many mentioned that they might have voted for the increase if three sitting supervisors had declared that they would not seek reelection.

This voter mistrust contrasted with popular support for William Popejoy, the interim county CEO and advocate of the tax increase. Popejoy, a former Savings and Loan executive and government outsider, offered his services to the county "at the right price"—for free. As he explained at the time, his interest in the job was fueled by "a sense of civic duty."

Although Popejoy's work earned him high praise, he was unable to convince the public. As he acknowledged himself, the structure of county government was partly to blame for the debacle: it was, as he said, "an accident waiting to happen." With no sign of fundamental change occurring in county government, voters simply refused to endorse the status quo.

Another reason for the rejection is that residents have yet to feel any pain from the bankruptcy. Government agencies, cities, and schools maintained services as usual. Most schools implemented budget cuts in administrative positions, away from the classrooms, and the worst-hit schools avoided default after a last-minute payment from the defunct pool. In many cities the cuts were unnoticeable, and losses were often absorbed by existing reserves.

We may well look back to the defeat of Measure R as a futile attempt to stave off the inevitable. While avoiding an increased sales tax, voters will likely pay higher fees for trash collection, libraries, and other services. In Irvine, where the loss to the school district was particularly large, local voters will probably be asked to pay a "parcel tax" to help fund the schools.

The implications of the rejection, though, are wide-ranging. The prospects of deteriorating schools and other local services have prompted local corporations to consider leaving the county. Lingering uncertainty could likely compound damage already done to the moribund real estate market, where some analysts estimate that housing prices have dropped by 5% because of the bankruptcy alone.

The county will also have to ante up millions in additional costs and legal fees. When in early July the county came to a last-minute agreement with its bondholders to roll over its $800 million debt for another year, the taxpayers shouldered an additional tab of $29 million. But without this accord, the county would have been in default. It now has time to develop "Plan B" for paying $450 million to its bond-holders and vendors and $900 million to its pool members. With a discretionary budget down to $275 million, this task will be formidable.

A variety of solutions will be put forward, including asset sales, debt forgiveness, recapture of tax funds, and possibly going back to voters for a tax increase.

Orange County voters may still approve a sales tax increase. They have approved requests for tax increases in the past and will likely do so again if two conditions are met. First, voters will demand accountability, as well as reforms, from county government. Second, voters must be convinced that this is a giant zero-sum game for the county: lower taxes here will be offset by higher fees or lower housing prices there. One way or another, residents will have to pay for the $1.7 billion loss. A speedy resolution to this financial turmoil is in the best interest of local residents.

We can look forward to fascinating developments for years to come.

July 1995

Bibliography
. . . .

Allen, F., and D. Gale. 1994. *Financial Innovations and Risk Sharing.* Cambridge, Mass.: MIT Press.

Altman, E. 1990. *The High-Yield Debt Market: Investment Performance and Economic Impact.* Homewood, Ill.: Dow Jones-Irwin.

California State Auditor, 1995. *Orange County: Treasurer's Investment Strategy Was Excessively Risky and Violated the Public Trust.* Sacramento, Calif.: Bureau of State Audit.

Fabozzi, F. 1993. *Bond Markets, Analysis and Strategies.* Englewood Cliffs, N.J.: Prentice-Hall.

Group of Thirty. 1993. *Derivatives: Practices and Principles.* New York: Group of Thirty.

Jorion, P. 1995. *The Importance of Derivative Securities Markets to Modern Finance.* Chicago: Catalyst Institute.

Jorion, P. and S. Khoury. 1995. *Financial Risk Management: Domestic and International Dimensions.* Cambridge, Mass.: Blackwell.

Miller, M. 1991. *Financial Innovations and Market Volatility.* Cambridge, Mass.: Blackwell.

Peng, D., and R. Dattatreya. 1995. *The Structured Note Market.* Chicago: Probus.

Smith, C., and C. Smithson. 1990. *The Handbook of Financial Engineering.* New York: Harper Business.

Stigum, M. 1990. *The Money Market.* Homewood, Ill.: Dow Jones-Irwin.

United States Congress, 1994. *Safety and Soundness Issues Related to Bank Derivatives.* Washington, D.C.: Government Printing Office.

United States General Accounting Office. 1994. *Financial Derivatives: Actions Needed to Protect the Financial System.* Washington, D.C.: Government Printing Office.

White, L. 1991. *The S&L Debacle: Public Policy Lessons for Bank and Thrift Regulation.* New York: Oxford University Press.

Glossary of Financial Terms

. . . .

bankruptcy   Bankruptcy occurs when the assets of a firm,
individual, or local government are insufficient to meet
the obligations to debt holders. The bankruptcy process
is governed by U.S. bankruptcy laws under several
"chapters." Private corporations have the choice to
either be reorganized under Chapter 11 or be liquidated under Chapter 7. Local governments can seek
protection from creditors under Chapter 9.

book value   Value at which a security such as a bond is re-
corded in the financial statements (on the books). This
may be measured at historical (acquisition) value or
market value.

call option   An option giving the buyer the right to purchase
the underlying asset at a fixed delivery price.

cap   This is a "call" option on interest rates. It provides a
payment to the buyer when interest rates increase above
some level.

collar   This is a combination of a "cap" and a "floor." It
provides a payment to the buyer when interest rates
move outside some predefined band.

Commodity Futures Trading Commission (CFTC) The federal regulatory agency established by the Commodity Exchange Act of 1974 to regulate futures and commodity option trading in the United States.

credit risk Risk that arises when counterparties are unwilling or unable to fulfill their contractual obligations to pay their losses. Also known as default risk.

derivatives Financial contracts whose returns are linked to, or derived from, the performance of some underlying asset.

duration A measure of a bond's price sensitivity to interest rate changes. The duration of a bond is commonly defined as the weighted average maturity of the bond, taking into account all cash flows, including coupon payments and principal repayment.

face value Repayment amount promised by the borrower of a bond. The face value, also called par value, is usually prominently displayed on the bond certificate. Depending on movements in interest rates, the face value can be quite different from the market value.

Federal Reserve Bank A federal agency, affectionately known as the "Fed," that controls the money supply in the United States. The Fed's mandate is to achieve low inflation and reasonable economic growth. The Fed's primary tools for intervention are the "federal funds rate" and the "discount rate."

floor This is a "put" option on interest rates. It provides a payment to the buyer when interest rates fall below some level.

forward contract A deferred contract in which two parties agree to buy and sell an asset at some future time at a specified price, called the forward rate.

futures contract A negotiable agreement to make or take delivery of a standardized amount of a commodity during a specific month, at a price established on an exchange.

hedging   The process by which traders try to minimize risk; opposite to "speculation."

inverse floaters   A type of structured note that makes coupon payments that vary in the opposite direction to interest rates. Therefore the market value of an inverse floater falls as interest rates increase.

leverage   The process by which a position in a financial asset can be taken without having to fund the entire purchase price. This is achieved by borrowing. The leverage ratio is defined as the total value of securities purchased divided by the capital initially invested.

liquidity   A measure of the ease and speed with which transactions can be executed. High liquidity implies a small spread between the buying and selling price, as well as large transaction sizes.

long   The buyer of a contract or security is said to be "long." The seller is "short."

mark to market   The payment of interim profits or losses on an open contract.

market value   Price at which two parties are willing to exchange a financial contract. It depends on current market conditions, such as interest rates, and is not necessarily the same as the face value.

margin   Performance bond that must be posted as a guarantee of payment if a position, such as on a futures contract, incurs losses.

margin call   A demand made by a broker to a customer, for additional margin funds.

maturity   Date at which a bond will be fully repaid or a derivatives contract expires.

mortgage-backed securities (MBS)   Tradable securities created by bundling home mortgages into a pool and offering different interests in that pool to different investors.

notional   The face value, or size, of the contract.

option contract The right to buy or sell a specific quantity of a specific asset at a fixed delivery price at or before a specified future date. Options are derivatives contracts, and include "calls" and "puts."

option premium The price of an option, which the option buyer pays and the option seller receives. For a seller, the question is whether the upfront premium is adequate compensation for future risks of losses.

organized exchanges Physical location where all trades occur for every contract.

outstanding The number of contracts existing (open) at any point in time.

over-the-counter market (OTC) Decentralized market where operations are conducted between financial intermediaries, usually over the telephone.

put option An option that gives its buyer the right to sell the underlying asset at a fixed delivery price.

repurchase agreement (repo) An agreement between two parties under which one party agrees to sell a security and buy it back on an agreed-upon date and at an agreed-upon price. In return, the seller receives cash. The difference between the original sale price and the subsequent repurchase price acts as interest on a loan, which, when expressed as an interest rate, is commonly known as the repo rate.

reverse repurchase agreement A repo agreement where the broker loans funds to a client using the security as collateral. The client is still exposed to the risk that the security falls in value.

risk management The process by which exposure to financial risk can be altered, generally using derivatives contracts.

Securities and Exchange Commission (SEC) A federal regulatory agency that has wide authority to oversee the nation's securities markets. The SEC's mandate covers the raising of capital, including the stock and bond markets, while the CFTC regulates futures and commodity option trading.

short   The seller of a contract or security is said to be "short." The buyer is "long."

speculation   The process by which traders try to make a profit by actively taking risk. Opposite to "hedging."

spread   The difference betwen two interest rates.

structured notes   This term generically covers notes (short- to medium-term bonds) customized to buyer specifications. Instead of a fixed-coupon payment, these notes offer coupon payments that change over time according to some prearranged formula. Payments have been indexed to interest rates, stock prices, exchange rates, or commodity prices, often with upper and lower bounds.

swap   An agreement between two parties to exchange a stream of cash flows in the future according to a pre-arranged formula.

term structure of interest rates   This represents the relationship, at every instant, between bond yields and the associated maturity. For instance, when short maturities pay much lower yields than longer maturities, the yield curve is said to be "steeply sloped."

value at risk (VAR)   A measure of the market risk of a portfolio. The VAR summarizes the worst possible dollar loss over a target horizon with a given probability. The VAR system has been adopted by leading financial institutions and might be imposed on all banks to measure their market risk.

volatility   A measure of the range by which an asset price can move around its expected value; also a measure of risk.

Index